The
Egotist

The Egotist

Laitman
Kabbalah
Publishers

JESSE BOGNER

The Egotist
Copyright © 2014 by Jesse Bogner

All rights reserved
Published by Laitman Kabbalah Publishers
www.kabbalah.info   info@kabbalah.info
1057 Steeles Avenue West, Suite 532, Toronto, ON,
M2R 3X1, Canada
2009 85th Street #51, Brooklyn, New York, 11214, USA

Printed in Canada

ISBN - 978-1-897448-98-4

Library of Congress Control Number: 2014945042

Design: Inna Smirnova
Editors: Paul Price, Mary Pennock
Proofreading: Norma Livne
Printing and Post Production: Uri Laitman

SECOND EDITION: FEBRUARY 2015
2nd printing

Table of Contents

How The Light Finds Us

The study of Kabbalah is not for everyone. It is for the seekers who aren't satisfied with the life they lead. They sense that the world has more to offer—a deeper truth lurking in the shadows, waiting to be uncovered. These are the people endowed with a point in the heart, a yearning that builds a vessel (*kli*) that allows them to tap into the spiritual world.

Only the Creator can decide if this wisdom is meant for you. We are all different. Maybe your desire to comprehend the meaning of life isn't developed enough to seek spiritual wisdom. Maybe you have sought wisdom from other sources and found they weren't for you, or that they may have ceased to answer your questions. A desire to know more could be pulling at your heart. If you are seeking to find meaning in your life, you are blessed with an important opportunity to correct your nature through the ancient wisdom of Kabbalah to find unending happiness, or at the very least, unending purpose.

This is not a story about a man making his mark on the world in any easily recognizable way. The changes I made in my behavior and the events that shaped these changes were incidental to the story. What happened to me was a full-scale internal change that came to me by making mistakes over and over again, so I could develop more colored and precise wisdom.

I now know the feeling of love as something deeper than romantic love. It is the feeling of the force of the universe clutching at your feet, offering a glimpse of the Creator.

The Creator (G-d) is the force of bestowal through reception. You will learn that by going against your nature to take, you will reconnect to your purest self. Kabbalah forces you to look deeply at yourself and correct your nature to receive the love the Creator wishes to offer every being on this planet.

From Below Upwards

For some time many of our greatest minds have submitted themselves to the notion that the world is a terrible place that only seems to get worse. Let's observe Woody Allen's attempt at describing the state of the world through the lens of realism. "I don't feel that I'm pessimistic. That's something I get called: pessimistic, nihilistic, cynical...I don't see it that way. I just have a realistic attitude, and the hard facts are so brutal and terrifying that each person has his own way of rationalizing that it's not so bad. But it is so bad. And the trick is to acknowledge that, and still get through."[1] We are aware that the world is unwell, that suffering is all around us. Some are better than others at disguising that fact, because our brain does not see the point of looking at the world objectively. Since human beings are incapable of objectivity, everything is viewed through an emotional lens.

Some are more honest about the state of things than others. Allen's friend and fellow comedian, Larry David, *Seinfeld* co-creator and painstaking observer of the minute details of life, confirms Allen's take on suffering. He elaborates, "I agree with that...I go through life feeling sorry for pretty much everybody. I'll pass a toll, and I'll think about the toll collector standing in there for eight or ten hours a day—how do they do it? How do they get up in the morning and go back? I feel sorry for everyone."[2]

The world has a way of beating us until we get to a point where we can't take it anymore. Our egos have risen to the point where we refuse to help each other. All we do is watch other people suffer and feel the same emptiness. Whether we have hundreds of millions of dollars (like Larry David), or we work in the tollbooth, we are disappointed with what our lives amount to. We want to empathize with each other. We want to find alternatives to our mutual suffering, but our egos won't allow it. We can make little, or even big gestures, to make others feel some solace in the misery that eats away at strangers and the people we love most, but these gestures don't direct us towards anything meaningful or lasting.

Everything outside ourselves that we look at as fulfilling is merely a distraction that keeps us from looking deeply within. And when we do address our internal struggles, we toil in our self-awareness. We believe we are unique individuals and use our self-interest to destroy each other and the world at large. In fact, the world that we consider to be reality is an illusion, blinding us to the infinite spiritual world.

Our lives feel random, disconnected and meaningless. Material aspirations are either unfulfilling or out of reach. We lack desire for anything greater than personal fulfillment. And once we are fed, we only get hungrier. There's a hole in the pit of our stomachs.

While this hole is impossible to fill by traditional means, there is a solution to the life-suck keeping you from getting what you need from life. You are experiencing life as it is and are ready to uncover the reasons for your lack. You may even sense that the coincidences that have shaped your life have some meaning you would like to uncover.

Many of us begin life with high hopes, but can't help believing we are somehow being cheated by forces out of our control. As we get older, we are hardened by these realities of the world. We learn to temper our expectations when success doesn't come our way. If and when we do succeed, the expectation of further success will ultimately be a disappointment, whether you're Michael Jordan or Steve Jobs.

This is because once we feel happiness it quickly dissipates. It is only natural. We are disappointed that we didn't receive what we were promised as children sitting in front of a television set that offered a version of life we did not have the means to replicate. The big secret is those who seem to have replicated a seemingly perfect life usually feel exactly the same lack. Everything that hurts us comes from the Creator, just as everything that gives us joy comes from Him. So, whatever we perceive as material lack is really a spiritual lack and vice versa until you attain spirituality.

As painful as it feels to our senses, this is an opportunity that gives us the desire to find a true purpose. We know that there is an abundant force that we can't seem to tap into. There must be another way. This can't be the totality of life.

We are compelled to both escape from and find meaning in the emptiness stirring inside of us. Unfortunately, without a method to channel these frustrations, we will not find an escape. We can study philosophy, psychology and religion to fill this hole, but for many of us this doesn't work, because it doesn't reform us in any meaningful way. We will ultimately mistake faith with ritual and stay blind to the Creator. We will never perceive Him. Some people escape troubling feelings by obsessing over sports franchises, and feeding on pornography, drugs, alcohol, television and movies. Others work until they're too exhausted to do much else.

While this may quell our loneliness and suffering from moment to moment, we tire of these escapes from the reality of our existence. Universities and great minds promise answers to the purpose of existence through intellectual pursuits. Intellectuals like Christopher Hitchens will offer, "Art is a reflection of life that gives life meaning...Philosophy will provide universal truths and reveal knowledge is the path to wisdom,"[3] while true wisdom is the sum of experiences and feelings. Of the few who seriously consider these matters, we are eventually troubled by their contradictions and errors in logic. Something is always missing, because there is no such thing as objectivity in rational thought that is always filtered through a human ego.

I, like many of us, felt intolerable suffering and voraciously tried to cure it. After studying a smattering of Western philosophy in college, I spent my entire adult life repelled by the concept of G-d. I didn't see any purpose in the delusion.

However, I found that rational thought was as flawed as the spiritual solutions to life's problems. I was embarrassed to ascribe myself to any answer to life's big questions that couldn't be explained rationally.

Thus, I was a secular humanist—the type of person who found meaning in novels. I spent my days contemplating the minutiae of human behavior, rather than exploring the true meaning of our existence. I was constantly entertaining myself with more and more difficult texts and films, flooding my brain with intelligent points of view in hyper-aesthetic worlds. It was a nice rabbit hole to lose myself in, but it directed me away from what truly mattered. Revelations or coincidences in my life were largely ignored in favor of a nihilistic worldview. When something didn't fit into my rational view of existence, I tossed it away like the garbage it seemed to be. When a great intellectual spoke of supernatural phenomena or G-d as an answer I assumed they were lying or emotionally insecure.

Alexander Pope once wrote, "A little learning is a dangerous thing." Misused knowledge may lead us to rationalize for the sake of greed and make us feel entitled to be rich only for our own benefit. And even if we do use that wealth for good, its joys will be limited, because it will be done in the interest of serving one's self. In the words of Jordan Belfort, the man who is referred to as the Wolf of Wall Street, "I mean, when all the bullshit was stripped away, nobody just gave out of the goodness of their own heart, did they? There was always some sort of ulterior motive, even if it was nothing more than the personal feeling of satisfaction you received from helping another human being, which in its own way was self-serving too!"[4]

So even if you do decide to be altruistic, there is a risk it will be a disposable feeling, because deep down the intention of this action will be to serve your own interests. The world seems to mirror Ayn Rand's philosophy of the individual that says, "The mind is an attribute of the individual. There is no such thing as a collective brain. There is no such thing as a collective thought. An agreement reached by a group of men is only a compromise or an average drawn upon many individual thoughts. It is a secondary consequence."

So even if you do decide to be altruistic, there is a risk it will be a disposable feeling, because deep down the intention of this action will be to serve your own interests. The world seems to mirror Ayn Rand's philosophy of the individual that says, "The mind is an attribute of the individual. There is no such thing as a collective brain. There is no such thing as a collective thought. An agreement reached by a group of men is only a compromise or an average drawn upon many individual thoughts. It is a secondary consequence."

It has become clear that equal opportunity is an illusion. Upward mobility has all but vanished from society. Society's progress is being hampered because the people who hold the levers of power, those with the money, live in a self-constructed environment where this idea of the supremacy of the individual dominates, to the detriment of everyone else. Kabbalah proposes we do the precise opposite of what our culture has covertly ingrained into us. Our society is built upon the pull-yourself-up-by-your-bootstraps principle that, "mankind is not an entity, not an organism, or a coral bush."[5] Ayn Rand's aforementioned perspective is how the world appears to an individual in his or her own experience when we are influenced by the ego above experimental data. Science has proved this experiential perspective to be invalid, but from our financial markets to our individual lives, we take exclusively for our own gain.

I was no different than anyone else in this manner, except that I had made the calculation that other fulfillments would be more valuable, maybe more attainable than money. I sought pleasure and knowledge, and because of my ego, I was a taker of the worst kind. I was an alcoholic and drug addict who appreciated intellect above even money. Though my pursuits of individual achievement and knowledge began fruitfully, after acquiring the abilities I had sought, my life began to lose meaning. I became so good at rationalizing my actions that my logic became a weapon to feed my selfish desires. I could subtly manipulate the truth like a criminal, though I never had to break any laws to feel like a fraud.

***

The great Kabbalistic sage Baal HaSulam once wrote something to the effect that we should be happy with the evil that unfolds, because the evil that doesn't unfold cannot be mended. Since this is the case, there is no need for shame when our flaws are revealed to us only in order to be corrected.

I had spent my life being ashamed of things that were truly useless to be ashamed of. I was stuck with my own flaws. I thought at my core I was a genius, but was ashamed when I didn't get great grades, so much so that I would avoid doing the work, so I would always have the comfort in my pocket that I could have done better if I had made the proper efforts. I had such a lack of confidence that I trapped myself in a pattern of embracing the selfish beast inside of me—that it had somehow made me more honest and brilliant and better than my peers. It was more authentic.

I sought authenticity and intense emotional experiences. I thought this direction would teach me something, living by William Blake's precept that, "The road of excess leads to the palace of wisdom." I thought genius was the result of an amalgamation of beautiful, weird, harrowingly intense experiences. I felt the sensations that geniuses had described—mainly with the help of drugs—but was too young and stupid to describe them.

Then, after college I attained a small level of knowledge and was able to express myself relatively well in somewhat compelling short stories. When I was young, I didn't understand the inner-workings of storytelling, but when I got older I grasped some understanding of how stories were told and the stories lost their magic. I still appreciated film, TV and literature, and of course I went through periods when I became fully engrossed in them, but they failed to shake me as they once had. Later, I was able to rediscover that feeling in Kabbalah.

Kabbalah was introduced to me at the time when my ego was inflated the largest. A few months into my college experience, my father told me he had been studying Kabbalah. Even though I had had a phase where I was enamored with the possibilities of

Buddhism, I thought he had lost his mind. I wasn't exactly open to a higher power.

With a tinge of cynicism, I asked "So you go and listen to someone teach you Kabbalah multiple times a week for three hours?"

He told me, "Yes," with his supreme confidence and I couldn't believe the words. My brother Miles shot me a look that said, "I know. He's officially lost it."

Though we were both raised as Reform Jews, religion always seemed to be something of an afterthought that was oddly important to my father who spent as little time in the temple as he had to.

My father was by no means a pious man. A ruthless businessman with an inordinately large collection of suits; my stepmother was known to call him dashing. We lived in the Chelsea area of New York City in a big, modern loft, and I attended The Browning School, an exclusive Upper East Side school in the mold of Gossip Girl and left that conservative setting to attend the ultra-liberal, ultra-wealthy Bard College, a place where to say religion was an afterthought was an understatement.

As a bad student, who had convinced myself I was the greatest mind of the century, spirituality didn't really fit into my worldview.

A naysayer to my newfound spirituality may argue that if I had been more successful in the world, this change would have never occurred and they'd be absolutely correct. If I were selling screenplays at a million a pop and beginning to direct my own films, I never would have turned into a Kabbalah student. In all earnestness, many of my goals have not yet been accomplished—none of my screenplays have been produced into feature-length films (though one is close) and I don't have tens of thousands of dollars in the bank, let alone millions—but in spite of this, I know what the result will be if financial and popular success comes.

I'm glad my life didn't lead me to endless fulfillment of my dreams and desires. I know what happens when my desires are fulfilled in the corporeal world. In a few hours, or maybe a few days, every accomplishment vanishes from my senses. I would spend days examining why I didn't feel the accomplishment, obsessing over its futility. Then I would move forward once again, until I was tired of the self-pity. This cycle of accomplishing a goal, experiencing a fleeting moment of satisfaction, descending into a vague, hollow place of restless disappointment, and returning to the beginning, yet again, left me with a lingering feeling of futility.

Another question hovered over my consciousness: If success were to come, what would I do?

I would create larger goals and feel entitled to things I never had before in the span of a few minutes. My ego would become larger, and I would feel an even more profound emptiness. The cycle would continue for the rest of my life, and no matter what I was able to accomplish, my life would be wasted chasing something that does not and has never existed.

I have seen it happen to friends of mine who have achieved, or been given everything they ever wanted. To a lot of the intelligent ones, the happiness is fleeting. My father's success in the business world only made him feel more empty, a hollow man in an expensive suit. He needed to turn to Kabbalah to give his life a purpose. For a while now, the wisest people knew this hunger to find something above material success was essential to a meaningful life. Art became a reflection of it. The American dream was dead, if it ever existed. And yet we—even those who clearly knew this was the case—half-heartedly pursued our selfish interests, because of our own egos and a lack of better options. I personally ignored this apparent reality until I reached a state of emptiness that was intolerable.

Our egos resist connection even when we know it is precisely what we need. This is the great challenge of making Kabbalah something that people can be eased into. How can I illustrate how ideas that physically repel us are good for us? How can I help others see that working against reception for our own sake, is the answer to everything that ails us?

Reception to Bestowal

My arduous study of literature, psychology and physical human interaction gave me insight into the desires of people. I knew what motivated people. I could read the nuances of the things they did—how what they presented to the world was a thinly veiled disguise to fulfill their secretly selfish motivations. Still, I didn't want to see this reality I was all too aware of, so I suppressed it in self-obsession and deceit.

Most of us have a conscience that knows when we're doing the right thing and when we're going against the common good. Even if it were possible to suppress your desires to your body's will, following a conscience is not enough to grow spiritually.

It's the tenet of every religion in history that doing good unto others will lead to rewards, usually in the next life, or the afterlife. Sadly, even religious people only do good deeds when the personal benefit outweighs the difficulty of the sacrifice. When the benefit is abstract, we do what we please. We pick and choose from what religion dictates we're supposed to do and feel guilty when we are unable to follow it.

We are not able to make these decisions, because our self-interest is so strong. More specifically, even when we have the right intention, our desire to feel good will override our want to do the right thing. And even when we do the right thing, it is only to fulfill our selfish desires. While our souls (conscience) tell us to do the right thing, our ego goes against it.

Abiding by the ego that controls them, the elites in society use their power to accumulate as much as possible. It's the very essence of capitalism. Democracy is built upon the lie of equality, but our nature is to not tolerate equality. We always want the biggest piece of the cake when our world is devoid of spiritual forces. That is why Communism failed (human beings were incapable of building a society of equality without the Creator since it is against human nature) and Capitalism thrives in spite of the troubles corporations perpetuate in society.

In the past, respect, glory, and power were not contingent upon money. Honor was above everything. During the last one hundred years, our egoism grew to the extent that we can see nothing except dollar signs. All spheres of human creative endeavors that continue to attract many people previously were once considered noble; things like poetry or scientific research made many artists and scientists sacrifice their lives.

Today, the arts and science are fully controlled and completely suppressed by money. Artists and scientists simply have to comply with this level. Sometimes they still experience self-sacrificing tendencies, but they have to suppress them right away. Artists and scientists are kept in narrow frames because they understand that their success directly depends on their sponsors' support and on the size of their bank account.

Nowadays, spheres of life that are extremely dear to us directly depend on money because prevailing financial systems buy them out, thus taking them under their direct governance.

All of the above also applies to mass media that completely depends on those who pay them.

This leads people, systems and corporations to act clearly outside the realm of morality. Commerce is the sole motivating factor in most societies and of course it corrupts the intention of everything. It shatters society. Every day we see senseless acts of violence in the news. The majority of the world suffers interminably.

But how can someone trust such a destructive force?
If there is a Creator, why are there mass killings?
Why did the Holocaust happen?

Sadly, when we are disconnected from the Creator, our egos expand and we do horrible things. We let horrible things happen. This makes it very easy to blame the systems—the labyrinthine nature of the government and the evil few who run corporations—instead of looking inward or feeling the dishonesty that is embedded everywhere. I was blind to the fact that people were good out of anything but a selfish desire to be viewed as good, or to fill their own egos, because I didn't want to view myself this way. As Matt Damon (Ripley) uttered after killing his friend in *The Talented Mr. Ripley*, "Well, whatever you do, however terrible, however hurtful, it all makes sense, doesn't it, in your head. You never meet anybody that thinks they're a bad person."[6]

I failed to see the hidden forces operating above what reason consciously explains, or to acknowledge that the perfection of nature could be seen as a hint that nature had some grand design. I was in denial of the fact I did everything out of a selfish desire to impress others. To the outside world, I looked like a narcissistic drunk (hopefully an intelligent one) with improperly channeled intelligence and a wealthy father. In my own mind I was an idealist, fascinated by the arts and aesthetics, on a path to democratize the art world with my now forgotten social network selfportrait.net. I thought I was making my own decisions. I thought that I was an individual of great value to the world. So I did whatever made me feel the most special, determined by the environment I was raised in and the people I was attracted to.

Nikola Tesla, one of the foremost inventors and scientists of the 20th century, clearly explains, in corporeal terms, how the individual is led by the environment he inhabits. He clarifies how our scientific understanding of the world is not necessarily at odds with G-d, what Kabbalists call the Creator or Nature. "There is no conflict between the ideal of religion and the ideal of science, but science is opposed to theological dogmas because science is founded on fact. To me, the universe is simply a great machine which never came into being and never will end. The human being is no exception to the natural order. Man, like the universe, is a machine. Nothing enters our minds or determines our actions which is not directly or indirectly a response to stimuli beating upon our sense organs from without. Owing to the similarity of our construction and the sameness of our environment, we respond in like manner to similar stimuli, and from the concordance of our reactions, understanding is born. In the course of ages, mechanisms of infinite complexity are developed, but what we call "soul" or "spirit," is nothing more than the sum of the functionings of the body. When this functioning ceases, the "soul" or the "spirit" ceases likewise."[7]

In Kabbalah the "soul" does not exist in most people. It has to be developed. Kabbalah teaches you to process what is presented to us as Nature intended. Once we can overcome our selfish tuning, we can escape the turmoil we have caused ourselves. We do this by correcting our intention, to direct it to the Creator.

One reason so many people go against the Creator is because He only reveals what one is prepared to handle. He does not reveal the sum total of His gifts. This is because it would take free will out of the equation. A person would not know the sensation of sweet without sour. There is no corporeal comparison to what spiritual growth has to offer. The world as it appears to us is no more than an illusion. There is an infinite universe we refuse to tap into.

However, we see the method of reception and bestowal corporeally in Nature. It is the formula that keeps the universe together. When our ego pushes us against the natural order of the universe, the world falls into ruin. By recognizing the deficiencies of our own ego in comparison to Nature, we have an opportunity to transcend the limited corporeal reality we are enslaved in. While this is difficult to discern, the influence of the correct environment can offer clues into an existence of infinite meaning. In Kabbalah, this feeling of warmth and empowerment is called a raspberry sphere, a little glimpse that can propel us to develop spiritual senses outside our rational view of existence.

Without spiritual development, we are not properly connected to the spiritual world and the Creator.

***

"Our five senses and our imagination do not offer us anything more than the disclosure of the actions of the Essence, but not of the Essence itself. For example, the sense of sight offers us only shadows of the visible Essence, according to how they are formed opposite the light."

—From "Preface to the Book of Zohar,"
by Rabbi Yehuda Ashlag

How can a person arrive at the realization of
the importance of the spiritual without having
experienced spirituality?

This realization comes to one precisely while in the state of a spiritual vacuum, when one is troubled by the lack of even the smallest perception of the grandeur of the spiritual. That is, one feels far removed from the Creator and unable to change oneself.

Whether we condition ourselves to wake up early, procrastinate, or eat too much, we already react involuntarily to situations based on past experiences. More profoundly, on a macro level we repeat the same mistakes. If you are a woman whose father abused you, your brain is wired to be attracted to abusive men, simply because it's what you know, and the cycle will probably repeat through the generations.

The environment you choose is the only choice you truly make. If you are in a place with positive stimuli, you have no choice but to mimic the stimuli operating on you and the people around you. Every choice you make is a preprogrammed reaction based on your past experiences. If you do not adjust your environment to attain the Creator you have no choices. Our nature is to repeat the mistakes of the past generations in the service of our egos.

Without a decision to turn to the higher force of the Creator, the most influential moment in your life will be the moment you are born, because it will determine the family you are born into and the environment you live in, leaving you enslaved like a machine responding to stimuli. While this lack of control is at first uncomfortable to imagine, it is merely a reality that is universally accepted by science. As Malcolm Gladwell observes in Blink, "free will is largely an illusion: much of the time, we are simply operating on automatic pilot, and the way we think and act—and how well we think and act on the spur of the moment—are a lot more susceptible to outside influences than we realize."[8] There is an inherent advantage to this. Since our unconscious mind works like blinders to our experience of the world, we are only able to focus on what concerns us from moment to moment. "We have, as human beings, a storytelling problem. We're a bit too quick to come up with explanations for things we don't really have an explanation for." If we are able to look at the narrative correctly, we can correct our desire for instant gratification and connect with others to correct the world.

We bear witness to the cyclical nature of mankind on a global level. The world has always been connected and interdependent, but with the advent of the Internet and global economic markets this cannot be overstated. We can now see the nature of the world in corporeal terms. The entire world operates much in the same way a single person does, which is why history is bound to repeat itself.

True spirituality is manifested by light that the Creator shades out until we condition ourselves for its reception. As material beings, we replace ritual with spiritual intention.

What is hidden to most of us is why we experience this suffering brought on by the Creator. The entire purpose of our existence is to reveal the Creator and feel the pleasure He intended for us, but since we don't know how to do this we suffer. As the maxim says, "Coincidence is when G-d (the Creator) chooses to remain anonymous." In moments that make us reconsider our existence, where we feel protected by some force outside of ourselves, the Creator is guiding us towards Him.

My Spiritual Development

I am not an authority on Kabbalah. I have not studied seriously for more than a year. I hold no degrees on the subject, and unlike Baal Hasulam, I never sought the knowledge of how the universe operates.

I was led gently, but then bombarded with truth, and at first it was too much for me. I resisted and protested everything, only to find with more life experience, that everything I understood about the world was a reflection of my ego.

As a former agnostic cum atheist, I was one of the many secular Jews inhabiting New York City. Before I encountered Kabbalah, I thought understanding the nuances of literature would teach me something, maybe save me from the acute anxiety I felt every moment of each day. I plunged into fiction whole hog just as others had once looked to science. However, both the novel and the genome would fail to give us what we lacked.

I thought my problems were circumstantial and had no spiritual explanation. Like many men of my generation, the desire to work in my chosen field was trampled by a failing economy, a lack of desire in a dying industry and the pitfalls of being overeducated—though almost by chance as opposed to any real efforts—and under-qualified for any career I had any talent or interest in. I wasn't yet a very good writer, though I was determined to become one. I'm still no Fitzgerald or Faulkner.

My liberal arts education never prepared me for my biggest obstacle, chiefly an internal battle with myself. I was unwilling to surrender my will to the Creator or anything outside of myself. My self-obsession and ego had squandered away my potential. My life had lost its meaning. I felt soulless, empty, defeated. In a state of depression, I turned to prescription drugs and alcohol, until I could no longer medicate the spiritual emptiness I felt. I distracted and sabotaged myself, because I was unable to cope with routine discomfort. My lack of will led me to the empty animal pleasures of excessive delights in food, sex and drugs, followed by self-centered fear and unsustainable shame, coupled with tremendous pride.

After graduating Bard College, I lived under the assumption I would write for magazines and then eventually as I got older would publish esoteric postmodern novels and be a New York public intellectual who drank martinis and joked about my life on *The Dick Cavett Show*—a show and an audience that had died in the '90s. Surrounded by successful people, it seemed like an eventuality that I would become one of them.

I was both gifted and inept. I had less respect for myself than I would for an inanimate object, but believed this lack of confidence would be corrected when I fit myself into a role as a famous writer. I struggled for about a year doing odd jobs before I began work as an intern at Details Magazine. Days later, four magazines at our parent company, Conde Nast, folded, and a lot of intelligent people were predicting we would fall next. A lot of people who wrote far better than I (though I was incapable of admitting this to anyone), and had the experience to back it up, would be out of work and turn to other professions. Publishing was, and still is, dying to the point that reading literary novels is a subculture.

There was very little laughter or sense of community at the office. Everyone was clawing to prove they had worth. Their egos wouldn't accept that many of them had become useless in the dying publishing industry. Two weeks on the job, I had been given the opportunity to fill in for the copy editor on an interim basis, and I thrived at the job, a day before what I considered to be my unjust termination. All I had done was leave the office in tears on my birthday, the day after my girlfriend dumped me. I used to cry a lot. It hadn't occurred to me my boss could smell the whiskey on my breath, just as it hadn't occurred to me that it was my fault my girlfriend left me for cheating on her.

Even after being fired, I never considered many people with better attitudes, people who didn't smoke, who sucked up to their superiors, and who were willing to follow instructions would take the scarce available jobs in the dying print media. I never put much thought into my motivation for pursuing the work. Looking back, it was a desire to validate all the time I spent developing my tastes. I wanted to advertise my superiority. This, of course, was of no consequence. What I had in literary talent and inessential knowledge, I lacked in work ethic, respect, interpersonal skills and humility. I squandered a beautiful, loving girlfriend and a great job opportunity in a single day. I was starting to get bitter. Why couldn't people see how special I was?

While there was no doubt in my mind the magazine had made a mistake they'd regret, severe depression had sunk me into a void. I didn't see any reason to get out of bed in the morning. My father had been transformed by Kabbalah. He invited me to a Kabbalah lesson, and with some trepidation I agreed to attend the nightly event in a building that looked more like a church basement than the grand Manhattan temple where I worshipped as a child. I was willing to try anything to feel better, except—of course—consider someone else knew something about the world I didn't.

I found most of what was said by the white-bearded man with knowing eyes to be profound, but I picked apart some of the arguments. Even when I agreed with a large assessment of something about the nature of the world, I argued it was incorrect, because I had no interest in spiritual solutions that satiated the desires of weak and stupid people. I understood nothing, because my coarse nature was unwilling to listen to anything resembling religion or spirituality.

If you remember, the one thing I knew for sure was that G-d didn't exist and spirituality was a way for the weak to cope with their miserable lives and the inevitability they would one day die. When it occurred to me this wasn't necessarily the case, my body physically resisted. I was both ecstatic and scared at the same time. My general disposition was to never listen to my father, especially when it came to emotional things. My emotional intelligence was far more evolved than a man who had taken care of himself since he was fifteen.

In reality, it would compromise my poorly formed values to give the group a chance, until a day later, when my father spoke to his Kabbalah teacher about my troubles. He encouraged my father to hire me. On the surface it seemed like a coincidence, but now I know better. Four years later, I now see it as a miracle. Coincidences are messages from forces beyond our control that we refer to as the Creator. If that sounds like something out of *Star Trek*, please bear with me. You are merely taking the position I did at first.

I did what my punk rock heroes never would have. Joe Strummer never would have taken a job he didn't believe in.

I was selling out for almost no money in the scheme of things, at least compared to my imagination when I would be the one lucky enough to take drugs and write novels about drugs like Bret Easton Ellis, whilst being as unmistakably brilliant as James Joyce.

Being unemployed and presented with an opportunity to get paid to write fiction, I couldn't turn down the offer, though I was so deluded I think my father had to explain it to me in those terms. Looking back, this was the happiest time in my life, before I had found the Creator and sobriety. I was able to humble myself enough to get my girlfriend back, made a very modest salary, and in my best moments saw the world from rose-colored glasses.

Only living without Kabbalah did I come to understand how big a hole it filled for me. I learned things, and then I looked elsewhere for answers. I knew our capacity for reason was not some pointless anomaly. I had to uncover a deep truth, but when I found the source to my answers, I hit a roadblock, because my ego and the substances I imbibed would not let me let go of my identity. I was shutting the point in my heart, the vessel I had almost opened to let in the Creator.

Like many American Jews, I thought the answer to my feelings of alienation could be solved in the material world. As an artist, I was convinced self-imposed suffering would lead me to truth that would lead to money and love. Suffering gave me the gift I had once effectively tossed in the trash. Most of us aren't so lucky, and admittedly, I had squandered it—the thirty thousand dollar a year private school, the fifty thousand dollar a year college, connections to the most powerful people in the world—in the service of my own ego and having a good time. What was clear, and I could not admit, was that everything I had done was to be accepted and later to be praised as better than others.

What most people in our society lack is exposure to the workings of the world and a willingness to accept a power greater than themselves. As I touched on earlier, it is an uncomfortable thought to know you have no control over your life, and usually it takes great pain for someone to be able to accept this fact. With widespread pain across the entire world, it is time for us to accept the will of the Creator and unite, for this is the only way we can heal ourselves and eventually cure the world of suffering.

Only when you become willing to forego your own egoistic desires and live life in concert with the Creator, can you achieve real freedom that will guide you on a smooth path to a life beyond your wildest dreams. The hardest obstacle for me was that accepting this kind of life forces you to let go of your own control to experience something much greater than you could have ever imagined.

In this state, there can be no return to egoism. Instead, there will be eternal existence in the spiritual world. For this reason, such a person will perceive the present and the future as equal, thus producing the feeling of having attained eternity.

Not a Religion

At this point in your reading you may be wondering how Kabbalah has come into being and what about it has transcended my experience of the world and how it will do the same for you. You may have picked this book up as a lark. In any case, you have some interest or curiosity in what Kabbalah is.

In order to understand Kabbalah, and more specifically, to be able to use Kabbalah in your own life correctly, it is important you understand some basic principles and historical explanations of the most powerful force in the universe. You must know what it is and what it isn't with a little bit of clarity. A small inquiry into the continuum of knowledge that is Kabbalah is essential for one to make a decision to study Kabbalah and trust the method it sets out for an individual. Every religion offers something positive, and most of them advertise their product as the only truth, but they do not hold the source to attain the upper, Spiritual World. This is the only method I understand that allows man to raise himself into the Spiritual World, an invisible universe above the forces our brain makes calculations to keep you from attaining.

Kabbalah has been kept hidden from the public for roughly the last 2,000 years. The very fact you are holding this book—not even a text composed by someone who has achieved degrees of spiritual ascension—means you are closer to correction (something similar to what many religions or studies may call salvation or enlightenment) than almost anyone over the course of human history. Before the mid 20th century, very few people who weren't Orthodox Jewish scholars had any access to this wisdom.

Only in the last couple of decades have secular people taken to the wisdom. Even though it is now accessible, Kabbalah is still only a little blip on the collective conscious in America, the country with the most developed egos where a collective existential correction is needed the most. While unconventional spirituality has exploded, the pure message of Kabbalah, the only path to attainment of the Creator is still a marginalized subculture.

Further, the popular culture stereotypes about Kabbalah make it seem like a cultish religion in the vein of other New Age and socialist spiritual movements popping up in America since the 19th century that gained particular steam in the hippie generation of the ˙60s and ˙70s and became commonplace in American and Western European culture. The residue is everywhere from the housewife who carries a yoga mat to the shop that sells healing crystals. All people seem to know of Kabbalah is that Madonna, Paris Hilton, Demi Moore and a slew of other unabashedly materialistic celebrities study it, and it has something to do with Judaism and a red string. Pop culture perpetuates this myth. In Gary Shteyngart's satire, *Absurdistan*, the plump, intelligent, but misguided son of a Russian oligarch studies Western Judaism and cites a passing curiosity about Kabbalah as the second most important feature of American Jews. When contemplating the job of building a Jewish museum in his research of Judaism, he notes that "I [he] learned about the average American Jew's curious if misplaced interest in something called "kabbalah." As for the Holocaust, few genocides were better documented."[9]

Jenna Maroney, the caricature of a hapless diva on the show, *30 Rock*, is a devout follower. Not only does she swear by "Kabbalah Monster," but chose it because "Kabbalah is a wonderful religion that mixes the fun part of Judaism with magic."[10] This is how some people in America understand Kabbalah, and whether they are fascinated or simply poke fun at the belief, all people seem to know is that it is an odd, maybe occult belief system that seems to have gobbled up people who would otherwise do transcendental meditation to calm their inherent uneasiness. This misconception takes away from what Kabbalah is capable of correcting.

Kabbalah is not magic. It is not mysticism. It is only the simple tenet to love thy friend as thyself, but not from a religious approach, because it offers a method to correct your egoistic nature instead of restricting it.

The predominant misconception people have about Kabbalah is that it is a religion. Kabbalah is the scientific understanding of how one connects with the Creator. However, if this, in and of itself, seems like a ridiculous notion, it means your thinking is squarely in line with the American zeitgeist. American society has broken from the traditional religions that were key to its foundation. While there are vehement "believers" that make up a very vocal minority and 80% of Americans claim some spiritual affiliation, agnosticism and atheism are steeply on the rise. This is a direct result of the rise of our egos. As a country, and now as a shrinking world, our desires have gotten so big we no longer can listen to someone else to decide our own moral obligations. This lack of faith in ritual is precisely why Kabbalah, the scientific remedy for transcending selfish desires into bestowal, is necessary.

Our society is built around the concept of individuality, and the value of individuality is a lowly one that is either confirmed by money or other perceived gifts of the corporeal world, such as knowledge, pleasure, or whatever else a person chooses to strive for. When our ego is not fulfilled by a material gain, we justify our lack of material gain. We protect it and blame the world for it and do nothing. We see the small chance of achieving what we can, and we resign ourselves from life. This is why many young people today have no hope. They go to colleges that put them or their families in debt and move back in with their parents. They work as little as they can, if they do at all. They see no profit in getting married or starting a family of their own.

While it is generally considered a positive thing in society to be true to one's self, our individuality is merely the sum of the experiences we have been placed into. We have no control over who we are and sometimes we are unhappy and destructive. Our belief in individuation has led us to destroy the familial structure and a belief in a Higher Power in favor of fleeting pleasures. These pleasures lead to self-destruction and depression. Millennials have unrealistic expectations about what life should be, and when these expectations are unmet, they cannot take it. This is true of the older generations as well, only not as pronounced as it currently is with young people. For these individuals, this will only get worse as the years pass.

In Deepak Chopra's book *How to Know God*, Chopra opens with the paradox of the world, that "G-d has managed the amazing feat of being worshiped and invisible at the same time."[11] Even amongst the believers, G-d is an abstract concept, devoid of power or real meaning. This is because G-d remains absent in your consciousness until He is awakened. Kabbalah allows us to contact the Creator in ways that religious people never could.

Even people without the path of the wisdom of Kabbalah recognize a force of bestowal being misused. While they don't have any answer to the crisis of the ego that destroys the world, they sense inherent doom manifesting within themselves in personal crises that religion can't calm. What they lack is the pure selflessness that Kabbalah makes us capable of achieving.

So the religious find pleasure in religion. They believe in following rules in order to go to heaven and the security that they are doing things correctly. And several others turn to Eastern religion and meditation to calm their anxiety. They perform selfless acts because of the promise that they will come back to them.

Many proud, often very intelligent people take the other extreme of not bothering with or believing in anything but themselves. The educated classes have shifted to agnosticism with particular fervor, and since Jews—according to the Torah, those with the largest desires, who were once the keepers of this wisdom—are, by and large, extremely well educated, they have followed suit. Christopher Hitchens, the celebrated, recently deceased author of *God is Not Great*, has gone so far as to say that some people, including a disproportionate amount of Jews, carry an atheist gene, which he champions as a more sophisticated form of living.

Hitchens' objection to religion is not particularly original. He borrows the same arguments Freud made when he wrote *The Future of an Illusion*, as have countless others have before and after. Gifted minds tend to cite the same points when proselytizing their atheism like a religion. I, as a former atheist and trained skeptic, would hear some argument about the subject of religion and immediately contest the words with my preconceived beliefs about the subject.

What Hitchens and many far more discerning minds than his are threatened by is that true spirituality is attained emotionally. The knowledge of Kabbalah is gathered through experiential discovery and someone who can immediately dissect the meaning of scientific principles and dissect allegories presented in *The*

Zohar may learn nothing of value. This is particularly useless in understanding *The Zohar*, since the corporeal imagery in *The Zohar* is a description of spiritual realms that are kept hidden without breaking the barrier into the spiritual world.

Spirituality is attained through qualitative actions. It is not attained merely by understanding difficult texts. This is why I urge you as a reader to skip over and come back to any section in this book if you have difficulty relating to a concept I present, disagree with something, or take only the part that you connect with. This is meant to be an introduction. You don't need to absorb and believe everything all at once. Do not allow it to repel you from an essential truth that may become clear to you further in your study.

Studying Kabbalah does lead to one overcoming sometimes upsetting things, because the process of becoming a Kabbalist requires correcting your nature, which tells you to run from anything that doesn't give you pleasure. To attain truth, you suffer momentarily as your vessels remove the layers of coarseness preventing the Creator from penetrating your soul. Usually sticking through the suffering reveals joy soon after, because you are finally existing in concert with Nature. In my personal experience, this joy is incomparable to anything else. True pleasure is the reward for your labor and the indication that you are on the correct path. This work is how you begin to communicate with the Creator in your daily life.

As I continue my journey on this path, many things I once thought were important, I reassessed as small, and many small concepts became important foundations of my experience. All I want this reading to do is give you a taste of the spiritual world, so you will be able to make your own inner discernments.

The next section will show flaws in humanist, atheistic thought. By refuting each of the broad objections Hitchens made to religion, I am attempting to make Kabbalah a safe study to those who contest organized religion. Kabbalah may even prove to be an acceptable study for the staunchest of the atheists who picked up this book to contest it. There are limits to what I am illustrating, because it is a rational argument about a study that transcends reason. Thus, this is not a spiritual exercise. It is simply an argument to show what Kabbalah is by examining what it isn't.

Post-Humanism

Kabbalah in today's world presents a post-humanist perspective. It recognizes that reason is a tool of the ego to fulfill egotistical desires. My commentary on this philosophical text only illustrates that Kabbalah is not a repressive religion or a cult. I am simply attempting to eliminate the all-too-evident roadblocks caused by misinformation about the study that is so dear to me. While other faiths attempt to suppress our desires, what Kabbalah allows us to do is transform our desires for the self into a desire for others.

Hitchens writes of the damaging influence of religion very clearly. "There still remain four irreducible objections to religious faith: that it wholly misrepresents the origins of man and the cosmos (1), that because of this original error it manages to combine the maximum of servility with the maximum of solipsism (2), that it is both the result and the cause of dangerous sexual repression (3), and that it is ultimately grounded on wish-thinking (4)."

1) Science

Since Kabbalah is a science, it does not misrepresent the origins of man and the cosmos. The Torah and *The Zohar* are allegorical texts, beyond historical representations. The allegories all tell stories about how men overcome their egos.

In my recovery from alcohol addiction, I found a metaphor that connected to my understanding of reality. It made me understand the perceived absurdity of believing in G-d and science simultaneously is a pseudo-intellectual argument that comes from the ego. It is simplistic rationality that doesn't account for reality. G-d and science are not mutually exclusive concepts. Was Tolstoy a fool to believe in G-d? Was Einstein? We don't designate the Creator with a body or an image. We just imagine a clear force that is equivalent to Nature.

Though not from a Kabbalistic voice, Alcoholics Anonymous made me aware of the existence of something not unlike the Creator, which was an important foothold for my spiritual growth. *The Big Book of Alcoholics Anonymous* speaks of misdirected reason by illustrating that "the prosaic steel girder is a mass of electrons whirling around each other at incredible speed. These bodies are governed by precise laws, which hold true throughout the material world. Science tells us so. We have no reason to doubt it. When, however, the perfectly logical assumption is suggested that underneath the material world and life as we see it, there is an All-Powerful, Guiding, Creative Intelligence, right there, our perverse streak comes to the surface and we convince ourselves it isn't so."[12]

Kabbalah is simply an understanding of how to use the all-powerful force of the Creator to our benefit as human beings. We please the Creator by enjoying His creation. It is an expansion of the wisdom of this powerful force. Kabbalah is a method for connecting and aligning ourselves with this force and rejecting the knowledge that pushes us away from it. Once we understand our reason is really our ego devouring our capacity to be reasonable, we can take actions to correct our own ego and the entire world.

We are living in a crisis of the ego, and only when humanity is able to correct our unnatural experience of the universe, will we be able to live in a harmonious world.

Other sources and researchers are offering examples of Kabbalistic principles in nature. We can understand that these examples of mutual guarantee are evidence that the truths of Kabbalah are natural and universal. Evolutionary biologist, Elisabeth Sahtouris, explains how the world operates in concert with our spiritual laws. By uniting and loving one another, we can transcend our egos, egos that she describes as individuation—the process of man living under the illusion he is an individual.

Only when people connect and unite with each other, like everything else in the universe, can we transcend the world crisis. We are dependent on each other in the same way our biological systems are, but our reason blinds us to this reality.

"The human experience of the universe comes down to unity, individuation which arises conflict, negotiations happen, cooperation is arrived at and we go to unity again at the next higher level. That's why the story of evolution is so important today to help us understand where humanity is and what is our next step and we're right between that competition to cooperation phase... Our cells have a much better handle on past, present future than we do in our minds. In the spiritual traditions it has always been understood that linear time is an artificial concept that we've imposed on the world for practical reasons of ordering our lives, but that the reality, the deep reality of the universe is an eternal now, in which everything is there.

"Now today, physics is showing us a non-local universe in which no information is ever lost. So we're getting confirmation of the old spiritual traditions, understanding that the universe exists as a totality in a non space-time sense and then we string out individual lives and experiences, including the entire course of material evolution...So G-d (the Creator) can only think about things that have been in the experience of the cosmos. That's why we're the creative edge of G-d, having the newest experiences that add to the total consciousness of the universe."[13]

In this way, science is entirely in line with our way of thinking. Our goal is to have consciousness of the entire universe. We understand that the man-made construct of time and our egos pull us out of reality. Kabbalah describes this phenomenon in a simpler way, explaining that we exist in a single, vast system, called "Nature" or *Elokim* [G-d], yet we sense only a fraction of that system, a fraction called this world. Observing Nature teaches us that all living organisms are built on the basis of caring for others. Cells in an organism connect to each other by mutual giving for the purpose of sustaining the whole organism. Each cell in the body receives what it needs for its existence and spends the rest of its efforts caring for the entirety of the organism. An inconsiderate cell that does not take its environment into consideration and harness it for its own good is a cancerous cell. Such a selfish act eventually leads to the death of the entire organism.

While our brains and societies have evolved and we appear to have dominated the trajectory of the earth, our progress is as destructive as it is noble. Popular science author, Steven Johnson, half-jokingly wonders if ants are really the dominant species on the planet. "Say what you will about global warming or the Mona Lisa, Apollo 9 or the canals of Venice-human beings may seem at first glance to be the planet's most successful species, but there's a strong case to be made for the ants."[14] This is because ants work collaboratively in a large system, for the benefit of a collective, instead of for the ego of individuals. If human beings were able to let go of selfish interests, our world would achieve harmony instead of discord and everything would be easily achievable. We have done our best to destroy the order of the natural world.

While it may be an uncomfortable notion to think about, the sea levels are rising and the cities that can't afford to raise their levees will be sunken under water, making Hurricane Katrina look like a trifle. Destruction is upon us.

Johnson continues, "Measured by sheer numbers, ants—and other social insects such as termites—dominate the planet in a way that makes human populations look like an evolutionary afterthought. Ants and termites make up 30 percent of the Amazonian rain forest biomass. With nearly ten thousand known species, ants rival modern humans in their global reach: the only large landmasses free of ant natives are Antarctica, Iceland, Greenland, and Polynesia. And while they have yet to invent aerosol spray, ant species have a massive environmental impact, moving immense amounts of soil and distributing nutrients even in the most hostile environments. They lack our advanced forebrains, of course, but human intelligence is only one measure of evolutionary success.

"Local turns out to be the key term in understanding the power of swarm logic. We see emergent behavior in systems like ant colonies when the individual agents in the system pay attention to their immediate neighbors rather than wait for orders from above. They think locally and act locally, but their collective action produces global behavior.

"This is the secret of self-assembly: cell collectives emerge because each cell looks to its neighbors for cues about how to behave. Those cues directly control what biologists call "gene expression"; they're the cheat-sheet that enables each cell to figure out which segment of DNA to consult for its instructions. It's a kind of microscopic herd mentality: a cell looks around to its neighbors and finds that they're all working away steadily at creating an eardrum or a heart valve, which in turn causes the cell to start laboring away at the same task.

"The great beauty of embryo development, the bit that human beings find so hard to grasp, is that it is a totally decentralized process. Since every cell in the body carries a complete copy of the genome, no cell need wait for instructions from authority; every cell can act on its own information and the signals it receives from its neighbors."[15]

DNA allows every cell in our body to work for the benefit of the other, but some flaw in our wiring known as human consciousness has made it impossible for humans to work cooperatively with each other in service of a larger goal. Everything is solved automatically when individuals mirror the behavior of ants or the cells in the body. We don't collectively know to aim at building an environment mirroring natural order, because it appears those who achieve the most are fueled by their individual egos. Only by existing by the fundamental laws of the Universe can we achieve its transcendent power. In this environment we feel the pleasure of existing by the will of bestowal and find ourselves more sensitive to the outside world and the people operating within it.

I first came to this discovery on a personal level, six months into the process of writing this book. After studying the material and living in Israel, I felt lost and disconnected from the group. While I sensed a power emanating from the study and sometimes during the morning lessons had the sensation of floating on air, something was missing. I felt like I may have been fooling myself. Maybe all these efforts had become futile. I was changing internally and felt at ease in many ways for the first time in my life, but I was bedridden with the flu immediately before the Congress. The Congress is a convention of Kabbalah students who meet in places all over the world and partake in intensive study of Kabbalah and connect with each other in a celebratory manner to realize the lessons they had learned through study over the course of about a week.

This congress was a particularly big deal, since it was the first Israeli Congress in years, and it was dedicated specifically to the study of *The Zohar*. In the desert, we all felt something changing in the group, and it became clear to me that what I was feeling was something unique. Seeing was able to replace believing. We'll delve into this further later.

2) Servility and Solipsism

Kabbalah does not require servility, as it does not coerce anyone to study the wisdom. There is absolutely no coercion in Kabbalah, because coercion prevents the utilization of free will necessary to connect with the Creator. Kabbalah is a voluntary method one must follow to achieve personal correction. However, skepticism is welcomed as someone adjusts his life towards a spiritual path. If you find studying with a group is not for you, you may seek other teachers and methods. Most of the students have already explored other spiritual studies and found this study was the only thing that didn't leave them empty, trying to fill that hole in their stomach.

However, in order to enter into spirituality, you must come to trust your teacher, the same way you would trust a physics professor. He is clarifying directly from the Kabbalistic texts of Baal HaSulam and other sages.

It is the exact opposite of solipsism, as it requires one to remove one's own ego to cleave to the Creator by connecting with others. The wisdom of Kabbalah is not used to assert superiority. It is actually forbidden. The study requires connection. It does not deny the material world. It just proposes an alternative to toiling in the suffering of it. Further, Kabbalah does not ask you to give up the traditions of your own religions.

Kabbalah does not take anything from your life. It just adds layers to your experiences. Kabbalah gives you receptors, what we call vessels to prepare you to receive pleasure unlike anything you have experienced in your material desires. The pleasure you experienced before Kabbalah is actually neutered by a lack of desire you cannot understand with feeling the presence of the Creator. Servility does not exist in Kabbalah. You are finally given the choice to experience the world the way you always envisioned. You are not bound to rules—you are merely taught to experience the whole of existence. In a way you become like ants, in that you are constantly working for the benefit of the collective and the Creator, but you hold onto your individuality.

3) Sex

Kabbalah does not believe in sexual repression. In Kabbalah, we learn that the human body is the body of an animal, and sex is a natural part of the animal life and the human life. A man and a woman need each other. Without the other part, men and women are only an incomplete vessel, constantly empty. It would be senseless to shame someone for his or her sexual desires, because these desires come from the Creator and we have no control over them. Animal desires for food, money and sex are fine, but are small pleasures in contrast to the infinite spiritual world.

Like many species of animals, men and women should procreate with a single partner and use sex to sustain their love. In couples, sex is necessary because it increases the connection between partners. By directing your sexual energy at your lover, you are not repressing your desires. As a vessel of bestowal you will learn that the purpose of sexual pleasure is to give your partner pleasure, as the physical manifestation of your spiritual connection.

4) Wish Thinking

Kabbalah is manifested in the real world in one's lifetime. It does not promise any gifts in the afterlife. It is the exact opposite of wish thinking, in that it provides a method to achieve a state outside the traditional confines on space and time. The feeling of eternity comes in this life. The soul persists when we're gone, but this does not mean heaven awaits us after we die.

Hitchens goes on to further articulate his misgivings with faith through the philosopher, Blaise Pascal's concept that faith is good, independent of results and the afterlife. He points out, "The ultimate degeneration of all this into a mere bargain was made unpleasantly obvious by Blaise Pascal, whose theology is not far short of sordid. His celebrated "wager" puts it in hucksterish form: what have you got to lose? If you believe in G-d and there is a G-d, you win. If you believe in him and you are wrong—so what? I once wrote a response to this cunning piece of bet-covering, which took two forms. The first was a version of Bertrand Russell's hypothetical reply to the hypothetical question: what will you say if you die and are confronted with your Maker? His response? "I should say, Oh G-d, you did not give us enough evidence." My own reply: Imponderable Sir, I presume from some if not all of your many reputations that you might prefer honest and convinced unbelief to the hypocritical and self-interested affectation of faith or the smoking tributes of bloody altars. But I would not count on it."[16]

While Kabbalah champions the concept of "faith above reason," this tenet is settled directly in one's existence. Instead of depending on something mysterious, we promise nothing that cannot be attained through a method. We take an active approach to spirituality. Instead of adhering to 10 commandments, or the 613 rules outlined in the Talmud, we follow a single rule: "There is none else besides Him." We do our work in service of the

Creator, by attaining Him in our own life. We must perceive the Creator in our actions instead of blindly having faith in Him. Simply by achieving this faith in the Creator and by doing acts to please Him, we are rewarded with spiritual growth and the pleasure necessary to move forward in our spiritual path. It is not something we wait for. We do temporarily have to believe in something with no evidence, but the evidence quickly becomes apparent to us.

This is because Kabbalah is not a religion. A religious person will pray for G-d to benefit him and the people he cares for, while a Kabbalist will pray for the revelation of the Creator. Studying Kabbalah was once and for many still is, a subversive act. The public wasn't always ready for this wisdom, because it directly opposes the religious view of faith—to follow clearly outlined rules to be rewarded in the afterlife. Society was once entirely religious and anything that contradicted it was a dangerous force. Thus Kabbalah was studied in small groups, oftentimes secretly.

All we are is the sum of our experiences. The only decision that a person can make is the choice of the environment they inhabit and affiliate themselves with.

Kabbalah illustrates how reason is limited, but we can see it corporeally. In a fairly innocuous example, when you look at a review for an album or a film, the critic makes rational arguments about why or why not they liked a movie or piece of art. We accept this is this case with criticism. What isn't clear to us is that this is how everything works. We like something and convince others to like it. So in arguing for or against Kabbalah, I am making a fool's argument. A really intelligent social critic will be able to use his vast knowledge of things he likes in order to give a work some sense of social import, whether it exists or it doesn't. Then intelligent people will argue over the point, but all we are really doing is measuring if our will to receive (our ego) is satiated by something. Every time one makes a rational argument, it only is in service of his ego. He is gaining something, whether this profit is easy to see or invisible. Good people are the ones best able to hide their innate desires from the people around them. You may or may not have accepted what I contest about the atheist point of view that challenges religion and by proxy challenges Kabbalah for appearing to be a religion, but all you need to desire to study Kabbalah is a better alternative to the feuding egos that cloud your world.

Attaining the
Creator

For centuries, Kabbalah was closed off to a few select students and studied privately, and while it relates to the Torah, it is not traditional Judaism. The essence of the wisdom is that love and unity are the foundations of reality, and remain as vital as they have ever been.

One particularly rebellious group of Kabbalists was the Kotzk group in Poland. They wore worn-out clothes and treated the outside egotistical world with contempt. They deliberately distanced themselves from others by appearing to disobey sacred Jewish customs. On the Day of Atonement, when Jews were required to fast, the Kotzk group would scatter breadcrumbs on their beards to appear as if they'd been eating. Rather than attract, they chose to repel people who had the inclination to study.

Even in closed off teachings, the great sages of Kabbalah (most notably Isaac Luria and his student, Chaim Vital) secretly created a foundation of texts that would one day be open to the public, when our egos had risen to the point of correction.

The time for that correction is now. The global nature of economics and the advent of the Internet create a framework for us to connect with each other, but never has the process felt more difficult. Our individuality and egoism has never in history hit such great heights. Never have we been so disconnected from each other. Overwhelmed by the scope of our industrial society, an endless stream of public information and choices of distractions, people are suffocated. We feel overwhelmed, and all we can see are our own desires. These distractions obscure the meaning of our lives, cloaking the Creator with flashy images. Many of us feel hopeless. When the Creator is disguised, our hopelessness is the spark that will force us to correct ourselves and ultimately correct the world. This is why we turn to spirituality. The rise of new age spirituality and positive thinking techniques suppress the human ego, so one can humble oneself to make life more tolerable.

Humility is not enough on its own. What Kabbalah clarifies is that everything stems from the Creator. It teaches you to have a relationship with the Creator, a sensation unlike any other. The past, present and future converge with each other. There are no longer any limitations. All the truth and love in the Universe are at your disposal. However, this feeling is not made available out of a desire for this feeling. It requires a desire for pure altruism. We are not presented with these feelings, only because if the Creator were to reveal Himself to us in all His power our souls would not be able to handle the pleasure and remain altruists.

However, by its design, attaining this selflessness is a struggle. If we were to feel the totality of His pleasure, free will would no longer exist within us. All we could is selfishly pursue the gifts of spirituality. We would lose the ability to be selfless.

It is beyond human comprehension to understand the essence of such spiritual qualities as total altruism and love. Even the existence of such feelings is beyond our comprehension; we seem to require an incentive to perform any act that does not promise us some form of personal gain. That is why a quality such as altruism can only be imparted to us from Above, and only those of us who have experienced it can understand it.

In the world we currently inhabit, selflessness is impossible, because it is against our egotistical nature. Fortunately, in Kabbalah, we know the cure. Whenever we unite, the serpent hides its head. The spirit of camaraderie has always been our weapon against adversities. Now we should muster it, cloak ourselves with it, and let its healing warmth surround us.

The Origins of Spirituality

"**K**now our brothers, our flesh, that the essence of the wisdom of Kabbalah consists in the knowledge of how the world came down from its elevated, heavenly place, to our ignoble state...It is therefore very easy to find in the wisdom of Kabbalah all the future corrections destined to come from the perfect worlds that preceded us. Through it we will know how to correct our ways henceforth."

- From "The Writings of the Last Generation,"
by Baal HaSulam

Kabbalah begins with Adam, because Adam was the first man who was able to see the world from both a spiritual and a corporeal state. Eve's biting of the apple from the tree of knowledge was the metaphor for the inception of free will. All our souls were separated by this egoistic act. We are all merely a disconnected part of Adam's soul trying to put our pieces back together. Kabbalah is the method to work together toward achieving the wholeness we see in nature.

As the story of Adam and Eve goes, there was no sin before Eve bit into the apple. Since everything comes from the Creator, he did not create sin. He merely revealed what was already there. Before Adam's lapse from the Creator, there were no impure forces in the system of the world. Adam's single soul shattered into 600,000 pieces. These pieces are revealed in vessels, points in the heart of Kabbalists, where the Creator can reveal Himself to man, above our egos.

What we fail to understand about the Creator is that he is an unchanging force that can be tapped into, to the point where we will feel absolute, unending goodness in our universe. The Zohar explains even the trunk of the tree tasted like apples, meaning that it was impossible to find an impure place in need of correction. However, the full depth of the Creator's power was hidden until Adam went against Him. As humans we are not capable of distinguishing sweet without the sensation of sour.

Adam and Eve's disobedience was the dawn of man. We are no longer living as animals. We have free will to connect with the Creator, just as we have free will to pursue knowledge, meaning in Kabbalistic terms, selfish earthly desires.

Free will raised man's ego to a degree that the method of Kabbalah was necessary. The first method of Kabbalistic study was created by Abraham as an antidote for the growth of the human ego as the Tower of Babel was built. He was the first of the four great Kabbalists who shaped our study. After Abraham came Moses. He wrote the Torah as a method for correction that was applicable for man to correct his ego in his own time. Rabbi Akiva's circumstances presented new challenges. Under Roman occupation, he created the law of love, to love your neighbor as yourself. After a plague killed his 24,000 students, the remaining few needed to update the message of the Torah to equip man to correct his own nature. For this purpose *The Zohar* was written and hidden until the world was ready to receive its wisdom. Rabbi Akiva's student, Rashbi (Rabbi Shimon Bar Yochai), and his followers were the authors of *The Zohar*. These men, who had attained all the degrees of spirituality, were followed and interpreted by many sages. But all those other sages lacked the importance of The ARI, Rabbi Isaac Luria. The ARI was needed to elaborate on *The Zohar* to make it more relatable to his students. His student Chaim Vital immortalized The ARI's teaching the method of Lurianic Kabbalah in *The Tree of Life* and other texts. Later, in the early 20th century, Baal HaSulam was able to elaborate on these studies to a new generation.

Contemporary Kabbalah is the result of Baal Hasulam's commentary of the ARI's writings and his writings on *The Zohar*. Baal HaSulam publicized Kabbalah as a means of correcting the world. He predicted World War II and The Holocaust, and saw the inevitable destructions to come if the world could not correct itself. He opened the study of Kabbalah to all, in order to correct the world, and saw this was only achievable in a group study, through his method of connecting with each other to discover the Creator and disseminating the method to the masses. Today's Kabbalists are studying and doing work to disseminate their wisdom in the tradition of Baal HaSulam.

Our experiences are no different than the great sages of Kabbalah in that we are all experiencing troubles that force our egos to be corrected. We are all working for the same purpose. We strive to correct the nature of man. While thousands of years and many great sages have contemplated the crises of their own time, every generation presents new challenges.

The wisdom of Kabbalah emerges when it is necessary, when the Creator chooses to reveal it. In our time, this wisdom is readily accessible, yet only a small portion of society sees any apparent use for spirituality. In the last few decades, this has been changing slowly, as Kabbalah begins to fall into the hands of new scholars who begin to learn the one truth of reality, that the Creator reveals himself through our connection with each other. Looking at this history, it is not important that you retain anything except for the fact all these men understood unity was the path to reveal the Creator. It is something great to aspire to that is in the continuum of a great tradition. More specifically, we must retain in our soul that everything comes from the Creator. The men who understood this principle were given the tools by the Creator to correct their own nature and the people around them throughout history.

These tools have been adapted throughout the centuries to fulfill the needs of every generation, needs that were defined by developing egos, natural phenomena, and technological advances. The development of man presents unique world problems that the sages have translated to help each generation.

As you achieve more spiritually, you grow more and become able to process the works of these great sages more deeply. The Creator reveals only what your ego is able to handle. He does not change, but your means of reception change. So the words of *The Zohar* may seem like a mangled mess to someone who begins the study; to a great sage it is beautiful language that opens up vessels to feel the wholeness of creation.

This sin of tasting from the tree of knowledge caused the breaking of the vessels of a single soul to all souls in the world. All the work of the righteous during the six thousand years after is to return and correct the single soul, as it was prior to the breaking of the vessels, before the sin of Adam HaRishon.

After Adam, this desire for knowledge of the Creator developed alongside the rise of our egos. Throughout the history of Judaism, unity has been the emblem of the Jewish people, exceeding even devotion to the Creator and observance of His commandments. Throughout the generations, Jews stressed the importance of unity above all else. The most important Kabbalistic principles are that there is none else besides Him, and that we are scattered souls trying to connect together into a single one. Kabbalists are people endowed with a point in the heart. The people with a point in the heart are those who feel this apparent disconnect, and see the benefit of working with a singleness of purpose in the wisdom of Kabbalah to heal it. Countless sages and spiritual leaders wrote of the significance of these two trademarks of the Jewish people, hailing them as the heart and soul of our nation. They declared that redemption was only possible when there is unity in Israel.[17]

There is now no genetic restriction. The lack is what propels us to the Upper World. The Nation of Israel was the first group of people endowed with a point in the heart, and since Jews are the ancestors of these people, many of them feel an innate guilt that leads them to the Creator. This is not only true of Jews in today's world. Our egos have risen to a point where all men have some inkling of a desire to correct themselves. This is why in today's world, people of all faiths are urged to study Kabbalah, and many people outside the Jewish faith have a point in the heart that propels them in this direction. We all need to restore the unity that will correct the world. The unity that gave Abraham strength came out of a dangerous explosion of egos in Babylon.

However, this unity would not last forever. Moses was required to share his wisdom in the Torah, and we had to build a Second Temple. After the destruction of The Second Temple, the prominence of unity and brotherly love peaked. The Babylonian Talmud teaches us that unfounded hatred and division within Israel ruined The Second Temple, but it brought us closer together. *Masechet Yoma* teaches us The Second Temple was destroyed, "because there was unfounded hatred in it, teaching you that unfounded hatred is equal to all three transgressions—idolatry, incest, and bloodshed—together."[18] Evidently, unity, brotherhood, and mutual guarantee is the lifeline that has spared Israel from affliction in times of peace, and caused great suffering to unfold when Israel did not unite. In these trying times of distended self-entitlement and narcissism, we need unity more than ever. It has to come now, at the time it feels furthest out of our grasp. Abraham carried out the same mission The Israelites had to generations later, when the Second Temple was destroyed. He was the first man to do this.

Rav Moshe Ben Maimon (Maimonides) describes how Abraham searched for soul mates to share his discovery. These people with a point in the heart were the first Jews. "He began to call out to the whole world, to alert them that there is one G-d to the whole world... He was calling out, wandering from town to town and from kingdom to kingdom, until he arrived in the land of Canaan... And since they [people in the places where he wandered] gathered around him and asked him about his words, he taught everyone...until he brought them back to the path of truth. Finally, thousands and tens of thousands assembled around him, and they are the people of 'the house of Abraham.' He planted this tenet in their hearts, composed books about it, and taught his son, Isaac. And Isaac sat, and taught, warned, and informed Jacob, and appointed him a teacher, to sit and teach... And Jacob the Patriarch taught all his sons, and separated Levi and appointed him the head, and had him sit and learn the way of G-d..."[19] This is how Israel was created and how it remained in tact until the destruction of The Second Temple.

It is unity, through which one discovers life's unique, singular creating force. In the words of Rabbi Shmuel Bornstein, author of Shem MiShmuel [A Name Out of Samuel], "The aim of creation was for all to be one association."[20] Considering the current global circumstances, it is urgent to unite as a means for attaining the Creator. Once all of us know and accept that tenet, peace and brotherhood will result naturally. Let us contemplate Abraham's existence and society that shared some of the same self-entitlement that plagues our world today. We do not understand how these great prophets and sages came into being—how they were so in tune with the Creator—but the foundations they have laid are essential to the correction of the world. We need to strive to connect with the works of these sages. Their works were directed at the Creator, and only Baal HaSulam's commentaries on them offer us a chance of understanding their wisdom. He was a sage so great he decided to lower himself to the level of common people to create vessels for attaining the Creator.

Baal HaSulam

The spread of Kabbalah that began with its emergence from the cave through the discovery of *The Zohar* and the arrival of the ARI continued with the Baal Shem Tov. Born in 1698, Yisrael Ben Eliezer became known as the Baal Shem Tov (The Master of the Good Name). He was essential in the dissemination of Kabbalah to wider audiences.

In order to achieve his goal of dissemination, he founded *admorut*, an institution that put into place a Kabbalah teacher in every Jewish village in Israel. Those leaders chose "the worthy ones" to study Kabbalah, as a way to groom the future generations of Kabbalists. These students would study the mechanisms and laws of the Upper Worlds to become spiritual leaders in the future. The writings of Kabbalah shed a unique light on history and can be said to comprise a history of the Light of the Creator.

Thus, for many generations, Kabbalah was studied privately, generally done so covertly, by gifted rabbinical scholars over the age of forty. Sages were born out of this quiet development, but none were so great as Rabbi Yehuda Ashlag, the great Baal HaSulam, who like the ARI began the study on his own. Rabbi Ashlag's commentary on *The Tree of Life* provides details on the stages, events, and forms of life's creation detailed by the ARI. Ashlag did a similar thing with Rashbi's *Book of Zohar*, where he took Rashbi's abstruse text and clarified it in a commentary he called *HaSulam* (The Ladder). This is why Rabbi Yehuda Ashlag is also known as Baal HaSulam (Owner of the Ladder).

By the start of the 20th century, Kabbalists openly called for spreading this wisdom. Rav Kook, the first chief Rabbi of Israel expressed this mindset very clearly in one of his letters: "I have agreed to disclose all the secrets of the world, since it is time to do unto The Creator, as it is required at this time. Greater and better than I have suffered nationwide slander for such matters, as their pure spirits pressured them for the sake of correcting the generation to speak new words and to reveal the concealed, to which the intellect of the masses was not accustomed."[21]

His Kabbalah teacher, Baal HaSulam, wrote profusely about the need to disclose the wisdom of Kabbalah to everyone, especially today. In his essay, "Messiah's *Shofar*," he wrote, "In my assessment, we are in a generation that is standing at the very threshold of redemption, if we only know how to spread the wisdom of the hidden to the masses...And the dissemination of the wisdom in the masses is called "a *Shofar*." Like the *Shofar*, whose voice travels a great distance, the echo of the wisdom will spread all over the world."

The legacy of those two spiritual titans has been fulfilled. Today, any person who wishes to can study the wisdom of the hidden, regardless of religion, age, or gender. As Abraham envisioned, our global Babylon can now study the fundamental law of life, without limitations.

"It is written, "There is none else besides Him." This means that there is no other force in the world that has the ability to do anything against Him...And the benefit from the rejections is that through them a person receives a need and a complete desire for the Creator to help him, since he sees that otherwise he is lost. Not only does he not progress in his work, but he sees that he regresses, that is, he lacks the strength to observe the Torah and *Mitzvot*, even in *Lo Lishma* (not for Her Name). That only by genuinely overcoming all obstacles above reason, can he observe the Torah and *Mitzvot*. But he does not always have the strength to overcome above reason; otherwise he is forced to deviate, G-d forbid, from the way of the Creator, even from *Lo Lishma*."

The hardheaded people Rabbi Yehuda Ashlag describes are those with the point in the heart. Writing these words in 1944, as The Holocaust moved along at full steam, Ashlag recognized a shattered world full of broken people. In this moment in history, it was easy for people to lose faith in the Creator. If G-d is good, how could He allow such horrific atrocities to occur? He needed to elaborate how we would continue to live as savages until we came to His wisdom, and achieving correction was the process of altering one's intentions and actions to be done in a way to please the Creator. To become like Him, it was necessary to correct our nature, by doing the opposite of what our ego tells us to do, connect and care for others more than we care for ourselves.

Ashlag saw an opportunity opening up out of these overwhelming disasters. Our egos had risen to an intractable point away from G-d, and the only remedy he saw was to demand the Creator connect us together to correct the world. World War II was the physical manifestation of a world crisis of an interconnected nature he had predicted a decade earlier. He felt the suffering, and the struggle, knowing that this was the time to open Kabbalah study, to reveal the one truth of the world. In doing so, Baal HaSulam built the foundation of modern Kabbalah.

Kabbalah teaches us how to correct our egos to care for one another. By behaving towards one another with the aim of pleasing the Creator, we are slowly correcting the world. The anti-Semitism that fueled the Holocaust and all hatred of people will be cured. The environment will be preserved, and no one will be left malnourished or poor. We will learn to love everyone, not in spite of our differences, but because of them. We will see the bodies of other individuals like they are pieces of our own soul, a single system that is the Whole of the Universe.

***

Born in 1884 in Lodz, Poland, the son of Rabbi Simcha Halevi, Yehuda Ashlag was an uncommonly gifted rabbinical scholar. At the age of seven, after protesting the limitations of traditional Torah study, he secretly began studying the writings of Isaac Luria (The ARI), hiding it in the Talmudic books he studied in school. He'd found the Kabbalah text in his father's house hidden on the top of a bookshelf. His lamentations were the only answer to the pain his point in the heart made him feel in the corporeal world. Despite protestations from Rabbis and teachers, he persisted to study the inner working of the Torah. Something drew him to the hidden wisdom, and it was out of his control to push forward in the study. Fed up with fighting his strong will, his eventual supporter, Rabbi Feldman, led Ashlag to Baruch, an unidentified Kabbalist who became his teacher at the age of twelve.

By the age of twelve he was already a Talmudic scholar and was made a Rabbi in the courts of Warsaw at the uncommonly young age of nineteen. He had a photographic memory and committed to memory the entire Torah and Mishnah. As a nineteen-year-old, he sat in the court of Rabbis in Warsaw and studied German philosophy in his spare time. In spite of this, he sensed Kabbalah was the only truth that could begin to answer his questions about existence and give his life meaning. It was always the main focus of his study, causing considerable discord between him and the other Warsaw Rabbis. His stubborn adherence to Kabbalah was tireless. Still, his study of Kabbalah was missing something vital.

Finally, he was able to find a teacher whose name is still kept in anonymity. "While still in Poland, he met an unidentified Warsaw merchant, who revealed himself to Ashlag as a Kabbalist. Ashlag studied with this particular teacher every night for three months; he said, "until my arrogance separated us,"[22] and the teacher disappeared. A few months later, Ashlag met the teacher again, and after pleading with him, convinced him to reveal an important Kabbalistic secret. The next day, the teacher died.

At the age of 36, like a new crop of Zionists, Baal HaSulam immigrated to the Old City of Jerusalem, armed with high hopes of finding Kabbalah scholars who could build upon his wisdom. Though he did not plan to become a public figure—it was his intention to create a leather factory—his reputation preceded his wishes when he could not find an adequate teacher and began to teach others. He wrote tirelessly on the subject of Kabbalah and his new method for connecting with the Creator through group study. His work was just a continuation of all the great prophets and sages in the Torah who had to overcome the egos of the people of their times, beginning with Abraham, lowered to the level that common men could begin to understand the wisdom of bestowal.

During World War II, Baal HaSulam asked the Creator to lower himself in spiritual attainment, so he could connect with all the people who were suffering. His sacrifice of spiritual attainment allowed him to relate to the people who had broken the barrier of spiritual attainment and give them guidance. In order to convey his explanations, he needed to delicately pass on his wisdom from an exalted place to one that would make sense to people outside of attainment. In order to do this, he needed to write in a manner that would not offend the religious or the secular, so they would be able to connect with one another. All that mattered was that everyone who had a desire would strive to connect with each other in order to find the Creator. Later, he passed on his knowledge to his son, the Rabash, who more elaborately adapted his father's study further into attainment through group study.

The Correct Environment

While a historical survey provides an interesting overview of our interconnected nature, and the improbable way these teachings have survived through the years, in order to tap into this genealogy, we need to start as individuals working towards a common purpose. We need to continue this historical mission. With all the knowledge at our disposal, we, those with a point in the heart, must study Kabbalah to correct our own nature and correct the entire world. It becomes most important we know what we should do, individually going forward to feel the pleasure of G-d. By doing so, we realize the ultimate, sole, all-powerful wisdom that will give our lives real meaning. The Creator is everything, and all joy stems from Him. In order to feel his joy, we must first turn to Him in our moment of weakness, demand Him, and then become like Him. It's a force that solves everything. When all our energies are focused upon this single goal, we begin to feel a profound peace.

Once I was able to sense that praying for others was the right aim in AA, I wanted to know why it worked. I quickly understood this was a selfish pursuit in order to make myself feel better, but I also knew that if I did this to the furthest of my ability to make the other person feel better, it eliminated some of the ego that was causing me personal anguish. Of course, my selfish intention defeated the purpose of the exercise, but it made me wonder if there was a way to transcend this. Until we are corrected, the force that controls us totally is the desire to please our own egos.

This was also true of my foray into Buddhism, where it was clear to me I was not selfless, if I was building up karma explicitly for my own benefit. My mother began the study, and it drove me crazy when she claimed to be selfless, while also speaking of yielding positive results from "storing up good karma." The teacher I saw would say things like, "The way to get a job is to get someone else a job. If you got the job any other way it was dumb luck, stored up karma from a previous life." While the result of this action was good, the intention was impure and thus the feeling of peace it produced was temporary. Kabbalah opens up a richer possibility of creating a relationship with the source of bestowal.

Kabbalah is the method one uses to build a personal relationship with the Creator. Especially in our contemporary world, we do not understand the necessity of the Creator, because we cannot see it. We were created by Nature, and it is the only thing that exists in the entirety of the universe. We are all capable of making this connection to the force that governs all. This force is the only pleasure that never ceases to refill itself.

Some of us will ask things of the Creator, especially in times of great need. This is a flawed premise. You cannot ask the Creator to help you through corporeal hardships without an intention to help another person or please Him. This action of asking is only

72

an egoistical act. The Creator, however, will lead you to personal hardship in service of your spiritual development.

If you are able to tap into the Creator's light, he will cure everything that is wrong with your life. You must transform yourself to a force of bestowal. You please the Creator by offering yourself the way He does. Thus, the only thing we should ask of the Creator is for him to reveal himself. Through your inner turmoil, you must demand it with our whole heart.

If you feel disconnected from the world, if you are sick, lonely, desperate, and if you feel like you are missing something everyone else possesses, you are seeing the world clearly for what it is. We are all shattered vessels from one soul, disconnected from one another, searching for truth in a web of lies. Your suffering is invaluable. It means the Creator loves you. You are not satisfied with small pleasures this world has, and you are being offered the most powerful truth in the whole of existence. It is a blessing.

"The worst qualities are envy, hatred, avarice, lust, and so forth, which are the qualities of the evil inclination—the very ones with which he will serve The Creator."[23]

Using envy to each other's detriment is the trait that our sages refer to as *Yetzer ha Rah* (evil inclination). "The inclination of a man's heart is evil from his youth. There is no evil but the evil inclination."[24] Baal HaSulam writes that the evil inclination is the will to receive. Yet the will to receive is the whole of creation, and man constitutes the fourth and most developed level of the will to receive.

Why then is our will to receive
the source of all evils?

The problem is that the will to receive on the speaking, human level is not static. It is constantly growing and constantly seeking more. Because we constantly seek more, we are always deficient.

The Holy Shlah confirms this Catch-22. "One who is not content is always lacking,"[25] and is therefore constantly unhappy and dissatisfied. Looking at our consumer society we can see that if we succumb to that element in our nature, we will be thrown into a never ending hunt for pleasure, that can never make us happy. Thus we only are offered relief when we pray for others. Praying for your own benefit only expands your evil inclination in the will to receive.

We are able to see the futility of reception easily in corporeal terms. The more freedom of choice we have, the less satisfied we are. We waste countless hours deliberating over the relative value of similar products and are never assured by the choices we make. From the fifty toothbrushes at the pharmacy to the thousand channels on the digital cable box, or the unlimited choice of websites on the Internet—literally a self-perpetuating manifestation of human desire—options paralyze us. Perceived freedoms become shackles.

We identify ourselves by the clothes we wear, films we watch, sports we play and music we listen to. We show off our possessions and tastes, either to be regarded as special, or conform to social mores to be accepted. The sad reality is that we did not make these choices. Our uniqueness is only a product of the environment we were born into. Our tastes are only the expression of desires we have no control over. Our natural inclination is to allow our desires to be dictated by envy, our evil inclination. The more we attain, the less satisfied we are. We try to attain knowledge, money and power to fill a hole that expands as we put things into it. The closer we are to our goals, the less satisfied we become. Even multimillionaires strive with all their might to make a billion. Someone will always have it better, until you correct your evil inclination.

Abraham understood that the evil inclination caused all the trouble among The Babylonians, and it would never wind down by itself. It's expanding to this day. Conversely, he discovered the will to receive, an outgrowth of the inflated ego that was fueled by the evil inclination. The will to receive was, and is, the only means for man to achieve adhesion, equivalence of form with the Creator.

The very purpose of humanity was dependent on what destroyed it. Therefore, instead of trying to rid us of the evil inclination, Abraham developed a method to correct our egos, to benefit from its seemingly destructive nature. Unfortunately, Abraham's method does not work in today's world. It was never intended for later generations. Egotism perpetually grows and changes as time passes, forcing us to alter the method, to end up in the same place of bestowal above reception.

When someone first comes into contact with knowledge of the Creator, they may at first be repelled by it. To be able to sustain a connection, it is necessary for a group with the same aim to be influenced by the powers of the Creator. When one submits himself to Kabbalah study either in a physical group in places all over the world, or even in a virtual group (alone on the Internet), he places himself under the influence of the Light. He has the ability to change his nature, because he has chosen an environment that strives to work generously instead of in its self-interest. This development is a slow process that is expedited by his or her exposure to the environment.

The environment is like a reactor, a great mechanism, a therapeutic section, or a whole hospital. It changes, heals, and forms me in accordance with the first spiritual degree. This is how I should treat it, like emergency help I need constantly. I come again and again in order to receive therapy sessions, and gradually I am cured. I hear more and more, agree more and more, and feel more and more. I see how previously nonexistent foundations are revealed in me, and I become more sensitive to the environment as a whole. I begin to feel special phenomena that come from it, different evidence of the presence of the Upper Force in it.

Gradually, this seeps into my sensations and then into my mind. New impressions become imprinted in my feelings, and changes in them bring me new thoughts that connect and accumulate into understanding. In this manner, I establish a continuously tighter connection to the Upper Force, which is revealed to me.

Superiority: The Other Force that Propels Us

The Torah extensively outlines 613 commandments. These commandments are restrictions on human desires, which are split into levels of desire. These levels are still, vegetative, animate and speaking.

The most basic desire in existence is existence itself, the still level, something resembling basic survival. At the human level, that still desire is being content with a shelter, even if it's only a cobbled together shed. This level includes the ability to keep warm, clothed, and fed. Just like inanimate materials, which keep their atoms and molecules together but do very little else, such a person will wish only to sustain oneself.

At the vegetative level of desire, a person will want to sustain himself to the same level as his peers. As all plants of the same species blossom and wither at the same time, such a person will want to be the same as everyone else they encounter in their town. His or her only desire is to fit in. If everyone is poor, that person will not feel poor, as long as his or her standard of living is on a par with the social environment. And if the new trend in clothing is to wear the left shoe on the right foot, the "vegetative-level" person will be more comfortable wearing the wrong shoe on the wrong foot, yet dressing according to the fashion of his time. The animate-level person differs from the vegetative-level one in that he or she begins to seek self-expression. Such a person no longer settles for being like everyone else, but needs to express his or her individuality. For the most part, this level leads to enhanced creativity and distinction in that person's discipline of choice.

The animate level is the most complex place that one can exist in without spiritual attainment. Here it is not enough to express oneself. The desire is to be superior. On this level, people want to be recognized as unique. In other words, we constantly compare ourselves to others. We only feel adequate if we are better than others, until ultimately we wish to be the best at something over anything else.

I felt this desire at a certain point in my life and was willing to let go of my family, friends and any chance at happiness if I could be one of the great voices of my generation. I felt a desire to make this happen, because I knew on some level I was better than everyone else in the world, even if to an outsider this assumption was plainly untrue.

With our current knowledge of human nature, we cannot avoid competitive, alienating attitudes. These attitudes stem from within us, in the fourth level of desire. We cannot stop the evolution of desires, just as we cannot stop the evolution of the whole of Nature. Moreover, if we are to achieve oneness—the purpose of Creation—we will need a robust desire working like fuel thrusting us forward. We must not diminish or oppress our desires. It will not ultimately be of any benefit.

As we progress as human beings without a method for attaining spirituality, desires grow until you begin to live on the animate, where you aim to be an individual of more worth than other people. Those with large appetites suffer on this plane of existence without being fulfilled by it. Kabbalah teaches those individuals in particular how to redirect their desire to the Creator, the sum of everything that exists in the universe and attain the speaking level.

As a writer, the animate level has always been the bane of my existence. It is the fuel that starts the fire and the voice constantly telling me I'm not good enough. Being a writer is a hugely egoistic proposition that requires someone to indirectly say, "I'm special. I'm talented enough to be a writer." How else could someone make a decision to do something that most people fail at? Living in the bubble of being loved a lot and being told I was gifted from a very young age, I lived under the assumption I was a genius and put people down every time the opportunity presented itself for my own amusement.

It was fun to play the role of the funny, effete asshole and get drunk to magnify this sensibility. In college, in a drunken stupor, I once told a girl with an eating disorder she needed to lose fifteen pounds, a day after I had heard her telling her girlfriend the same thing. It was cruel, but I lived under a delusion that I was a close companion of F. Scott Fitzgerald, Charles Baudelaire, David Bowie and Gustav Flaubert, pedantically telling stories about them as if they were my peers. I didn't take objective reality, or the feelings of those in my circle seriously. People found the mess funny, and they appreciated me as someone of relative intelligence, who was funny and a good friend until I had taken one too many drinks, snorted a few too many lines or forced an exit from anything resembling a good time.

My desire to be special had turned me into a difficult, unlikable person, but it also established me as a character on my college campus. I had a lot of friends, even though those people who weren't my friends thought of me as an asshole. If everybody likes you, you can't be much of a man, I told myself. While I was doing a poor job with the writing part of becoming a writer in my early college days, I was developing a reputation as a hilarious, if difficult, party companion in elite social circles, and it made sense to me; I was special in the way Ernest Hemingway was special. So what if I woke up with a hangover hating myself most mornings. Did it matter that I was unable to sustain a relationship with a girl for more than a few nights, or that I always seemed to be broke and apologizing for something? I was accumulating the sort of experiences that glamorous literary types always had done before me, and I was gaining access to the kinds of stories that cultured New Yorkers would read about, while I read difficult novels and felt a connection to literary works and films that had explained why I existed on this planet.

It was a certainty that my work as a drunken caricature of myself would one day fill a literary icon's Wikipedia page with anecdotes about drug use and dating pseudo celebrities. I didn't realize that this large ego was a result of having no confidence, that all inflated egos were the result of insecurity, that even Ernest Hemingway, the man who read the work of his "competition" before he wrote, had killed himself, not because he had depth, but because he hated himself. These, and countless other writers were commenting on the emptiness of their existence and of existence in general.

By the 1920s it had become fashionable to write books about the falseness of The American Dream. Hemingway's friend and rival—a man who drank himself to death—F. Scott Fitzgerald closes *The Great Gatsby*, imagining what America was like, before

European economic interests that gave way to American greed destroyed what felt like a second Eden.

"And as the moon rose higher the inessential houses began to melt away until gradually I became aware of the old island here that flowered once for Dutch sailors' eyes – a fresh, green breast of the new world. Its vanished trees, the trees that had made way for Gatsby's house, had once pandered in whispers to the last and greatest of all human dreams; for a transitory enchanted moment man must have held his breath in the presence of this continent, compelled into an aesthetic contemplation he neither understood nor desired, face to face for the last time in history with something commensurate to his capacity for wonder."[26]

The American Dream felt beautiful, but it has been flawed since its inception. What Fitzgerald beautifully illustrates is that when man fights against nature, he is essentially destroying the place he lives in and through this process destroys his own nature. America is a nation that has risen on a path to its own destruction, much like our own egos.

In the 1950s, when *The Great Gatsby* was first made required reading for every American student, existential problems had already caused widespread depression in America, the most developed country and Europe, a place that had mostly restored itself from the wreckage of World War II. Appliances gave housewives more free time to invent psychological problems. It was becoming apparent The American Dream had some holes we couldn't fill with convenience and commerce. *Death of a Salesman*, maybe the greatest American play, was written in the 50s, expressly about the tragedy of this myth of American superiority. Later, the hippies, with some awareness of the futility of American life, decided to take drugs and drop out of conventional life, only to later live very much the way their parents did with even more well-documented, openly celebrated self-centered neuroses.

Economically this is no longer an option for the unemployable majority of young Americans. Today, as the middle class is on the verge of extinction, only the very rich seem to believe in these values, and even they don't believe money will bring them happiness. Once they attain material superiority, they turn to spiritually as a means of filling the holes inside themselves and hold onto the wealth that eventually enslaves them.

Fitzgerald opened *Gatsby* with the character Nick Carraway, acknowledging, "In my younger and more vulnerable years my father gave me some advice that I've been turning over in my mind ever since. "Whenever you feel like criticizing any one," he told me, "just remember that all the people in this world haven't had the advantages that you've had."[27]

As fairly educated people, many of us have the material advantages he is describing, but beyond that, we have the ultimate advantage. We have the keys to save our society from ourselves. The world's decadence rivals and probably eclipses that of Egypt, Rome, and Babylon. There is so much violence, distrust, competition, and exploitation in society that it is on the verge of imploding. Like Carraway, it is our job to empathize with those who suffer, share our method, even as others blame us for their suffering in a crumbling society. The empires have fallen and continue to fall in service of individual egos just as it had at The Tower of Babel in Abraham's time.

Following his confrontation with King Nimrod, Abraham took his family, his students, and his possessions and fled from Babylon. Along the way he collected people who agreed with his message. When faced with egotism, they united above it. This is precisely what we should aim to do. We need to direct the world towards connection before we eat each other up. By creating a force of connection, we will be able to overcome the force of the ego with *The Zohar* and the force of bestowal. The book has been closed off from the public for two thousand years for this precise purpose.

Abraham's group succeeded in uniting and grew into what became the people of Israel, a nation whose common trait was the desire for the Creator. Through unity, Israel developed a method to shift one's thinking from "me" mode to "we" mode, revealing perception of the "One" [the Creator]. While Israel was going from strength to strength by employing unity over egoism, the rest of the world was experiencing episodes of ebb and flow. With empires rising and falling, the hedonistic culture of self-indulgence assumed predominance. For this reason, even today, in the most hedonistic of all eras, Abraham's monotheism is the predominant spiritual force.

Today, people understand that the only way to avert a global catastrophe is to unite. We are interdependent, and thus united in global systems. However, to the extent that we are connected, we are also emotionally alienated. This causes us to resent the globalized world. This is specifically truest in economic terms, where interdependent countries blame other countries for their hardships.

Today, nearly 4,000 years after Abraham's escape from Babylon, the world is ready to listen. We have all suffered enough, and we are too smart to think we can make it on our own, that we can show Mother Nature, or G-d, that we don't need Her, because we are stronger and wiser.

The Realization of Bestowal

In today's world, the obtainment of social cohesion is of paramount importance. We might consider the revelation of the Creator an accessory, were it not for the fact that the Creator is the quality of bestowal, a trait without which we will never achieve unity, never mending the global rift threatening to wrench the world into global warfare. This is why it is vital that we expedite the spread of Abraham's method for achieving unity through equivalence of form. To do that, we must first abandon a vital notion in our society—the idea that we have free choice.

Science proves there is no such thing as free choice, the way many of us believe in it, confirming the Kabbalistic belief system's two thousand year old method. In recent years, data that proves our dependence on society has been piling up. These studies show that not only our sustenance depends on society, but also even our thoughts, aspirations, and chances of success in life. In fact, even the very definition of success is subject to the whims of the society one inhabits.

In 2009, *The New York Times* published a story titled, "Are Your Friends Making You Fat?" by Clive Thompson.[28] In his story the lives of 15,000 people were documented and registered periodically over fifty years. Thompson observed, "that good behaviors—like quitting smoking or staying slender or being happy—pass from friend to friend almost as if they were contagious viruses."

In recent years neuroscientists have been obsessed with mirror-neurons, cells located in a region between the prefrontal and motor cortices of the brain. These cells are involved in preparing and executing limb movements. However, according to a story published in *Psychology Today*, they also play a vital role in our social interconnection. "In 2000, Vilayanur Ramachandran, the charismatic neuroscientist, made a bold prediction: 'mirror neurons will do for psychology what DNA did for biology.' ...For many, they have come to represent all that makes us human.

"He argues that mirror neurons underlie empathy, allowing us to imitate other people. That they accelerated the evolution of the brain, that they help explain the origin of language, and most impressively of all, that they prompted the great leap forward in human culture that happened about 60,000 years ago. 'We could say mirror neurons served the same role in early hominine evolution as the Internet, Wikipedia, and blogging do today.'

"Ramachandran is not alone. Writing for *The Times* (London) in 2009 about our interest in the lives of celebrities, the eminent philosopher AC Grayling traced it all back to those mirror neurons. 'We have a great gift for empathy,' he wrote. 'This is a biologically evolved capacity, as shown by the function of 'mirror neurons'.' In the same newspaper this year, Eva Simpson wrote on why people were so moved when Tennis champ Andy Murray broke down in tears. ...'Blame mirror neurons, brain cells that make us react in the same way as someone we're watching.' In a *The New York Times* article in 2007, about one man's heroic actions to save another, those cells featured again: 'people have 'mirror neurons,' Cara Buckley wrote, 'which make them feel what someone else is experiencing.'"[29]

According to psychologist Christian Jarrett, it seems that "mirror neurons play a *causal* role in allowing us to understand the goals behind other people's actions. By representing other people's actions in the movement-pathways of our own brain, so the reasoning goes, these cells provide us with an instant simulation of their intentions—a highly effective foundation for empathy."[30]

While there are quite a few dissenters to the theories surrounding mirror-neurons, it is clear that our bodies dedicate portions of the brain explicitly for communication with others. In that manner, we physically connect with others by locking eyes, without any physical contact. In a sense, these cells validate the words of Christakis and Fowler, "The great project of the twenty-first century—understanding how the whole of humanity comes to be greater than the sum of its parts—is just beginning. Like an awakening child, the human super organism is becoming self-aware, and this will surely help us achieve our goals."[31]

Similarly in Babylon, Abraham was able to use self-awareness to connect his followers towards the Creator in their thoughts and actions. After his expulsion from Babylon, Abraham established an isolated society that moved as a group and functioned in mutual guarantee. He created a social environment that supported bonding, unity, and cohesion, and attached all those elements to the acquisition of the quality of bestowal, the Creator. Our task today is to do just that, but on a global scale.

Because we are aware that people are only a small part of a much larger super organism, it is clear that we must function as one, in a mutually responsible manner. But since we cannot teach the entire world how to function, we must influence the world by example. The world will be forced to follow a better society by "imitation and influence." After all, when people see a good idea, they naturally embrace it, since if the world senses it will make their lives better, they will intuitively follow this path out of their will to receive.

Baal Hasulam, decades before its emergence as a scientific study, understood the science of mirror neurons intuitively. He knew that Kabbalah had the power to reconfigure the brain to a higher purpose. The environment and the surrounding light have the power to end all suffering in the world. When people work towards connection over competition, every individual problem will easily be solved. There will be no benefit to the sickness of asserting one's superiority. In his essay, "The Freedom,"[32] Baal HaSulam discusses extensively the structure of the human psyche, and what we need to focus on in order to achieve a lasting change in our societies. Through a long analysis of the interplay between the heredity and the environment, Ashlag explains that four factors combine to make us who we are:

1. Genes;
2. The way our genes manifest through life;
3. The direct environment, such as family and friends;
4. Indirect environment, such as the media, the economy, or friends of friends.

(Italicized emphases added by the editor) "It is true that the desire has no freedom. Rather, it is operated by the above four factors [Genes; how they manifest, direct environment, indirect environment]. And one is *compelled* to think and examine as they suggest, *denied of any strength to criticize or change...*" In the subsequent section, "The Necessity to Choose a Good Environment," he adds, "As we have seen, it is a simple thing, and should be observed by each and every one of us. For although everyone has one's own source, the forces are revealed openly only through the environment one is in."[33]

This may sound deterministic, because if our environment governs us completely, then freedom of choice would not exist. Nothing we would choose to do would matter. And yet, writes Baal HaSulam, we can and must choose our environment very carefully. We can choose a correct environment for spiritual development where we can transcend our self-fulfilling nature. "There is freedom for the will to initially choose such an environment...that impart to one good concepts. If one does not do that, but is willing to enter any environment that one comes by...one is bound to fall into a bad environment...In consequence, one will be forced into foul concepts..." Such a person, he concludes, "will certainly be punished, not because of one's evil thoughts or deeds, in which one has no choice, but because of not choosing to be in a good environment, for in that there is definitely a choice. Therefore, one who strives to continually choose a better environment is worthy of praise and reward. But here, too, it is not because of one's good thoughts and deeds, ...but because of one's efforts to acquire a good environment, which brings...good thoughts."[34]

The choice of whether we act out one extreme or the other, or any mixture of the two, depends not on whether we choose to be one way or another, but on the social environment we fashion for ourselves. Every parent instinctively warns one's children to stay away from the bad kids in the neighborhood. The awareness of the influence of environment is inherent in our instincts. To use this information for the improvement of the world, we must start designing a new paradigm of thinking for ourselves. Mutual guarantee (Arvut) has the power to shift the trajectory of the global world. All we need is the right force of social contagion.

Since we do not choose our parents, we cannot control our gene pool. But our genes are merely the "potential we," not the actual we that will eventually manifest as when we grow up. The actual "we" consist of all four factors. Moreover, the latter two—which relate to the environment—affect and change our genes to suit our environment.

Dr. Lars Olov Bygren, a preventive-health specialist, documented how genes change through environmental effects. Dr. Bygren researched the long-term effects that extreme feast and famine years had on the residents of an isolated Swedish village. Dr. Bygren observed more than dietary trends, focusing on, "whether that effect could start even *before* [emphasis added] pregnancy: Could parents' experiences early in their lives somehow change the traits they passed to their offspring?"[35] "It was a heretical idea," writes Mr. Cloud. "After all, we have had a long-standing deal with biology: whatever choices we make during our lives might ruin our short-term memory or make us fat or hasten death, but they won't change our genes—our actual DNA. Which meant that when we had kids of our own, the genetic slate would be wiped clean.

"What's more, any such effects of nurture (environment) on a species' nature (genes) were not supposed to happen so quickly. Charles Darwin's *On the Origin of Species*...taught us that evolutionary changes take place over many generations and through millions of years of natural selection. But Bygren and other scientists have now amassed historical evidence suggesting that powerful environmental conditions...can leave an imprint on the genetic material in eggs and sperm. These genetic imprints can short-circuit evolution, passing along new traits in a single generation."[36]

In other words, Rabbi Akiva's maxim, "Love your neighbor as yourself," must take shape and mold into a way of life for society. In an era of overlapping global crises, the world is in desperate need of a silver lining. Any hope at creating a harmonious future for our global society is entirely dependent on *arvut*.

I never expected the sensation of *arvut* to be revealed in me. When I was able to adjust my ego to recognize this from a personal standpoint, and other shortcomings I had in my own life, I began to connect with the group, care for the others and see them caring for me. However, I still wanted Kabbalah to only leave a small impression on my life. I wanted my life to largely follow the same course, and be satisfied with the minimal efforts I could afford to commit to spirituality, without losing any part of my precious individuality. I wanted Kabbalah to be a minor blip on my consciousness that would help me clarify some of the mysteries of the world, while I continued to lead a selfish existence of partying and living off my father and my social currency—my proximity to cooler and more famous individuals than me who were by and large as disconnected from nature as I was.

It was not as easy as I believed. The process left an indelible impression, where I began adjusting myself to the Creator's will unconsciously. What I didn't fully understand was that "there is none else besides Him," and that by exposing myself to His truth, more would be revealed to me about myself than ever before. Still, this was not to be an easy undertaking.

I had to go undergo huge changes to adjust myself to the state I was in. Knowledge of the Creator showed me the dark cloud of spiritual emptiness I felt. The first thing that happened was that I abused drugs and alcohol to avoid the guilt I felt about everyone and everything. I was afraid of my own shadow. My girlfriend left me. I was kicked out of my father's house, where I ended up when I had lost my apartment and my restaurant job. I had to run to my mother and beg her to let me stay in her apartment in between subletters, before I scrounged up enough money to find a place to stay.

A few short months later, by the grace of the Creator, I ended up in an environment with the power to correct my genes out of self-interest to bestowal. That place was my Kabbalah study group, the one environment in the universe that I know of that systematically builds an environment of mutual guarantee to correct individuals into vessels of bestowal.

Imagine the ills of society vanished. Just imagine a place where neighbors care for each other just as they care for their own children. Maybe this proposition is too difficult to envision. You may be thinking, "Why would someone want to do something that will do nothing for me? You may immediately be suspicious of them. What are they getting out of this kindness?"

When you are able to shed your ego, the Creator provides sensations of joy that will startle and excite you. When you begin to act for the benefit of others, your body will resist. You will be irritated and repelled. You will look at the people you're trying to help like they're weak and stupid. This is because you're going against your nature. Then after resigning your ego at the expense of yourself, sometime in the future you will be rewarded, maybe just after you've given up all hope that this selflessness has any value or meaning. You will slowly become a different person. You will begin to love everyone, and you will feel everyone loves you. Everything that sickened you will become an opportunity to correct selfishness in the service of connection. Your world will turn upside down, and you will become aware that everything you did for yourself was a wasted action. You will feel an inner calmness and a sense of purpose.

The End of Empty Pleasures

Back in New York, I had never felt so alone. I was angry at the world, a world that had failed to recognize my greatness. My inability to cope with discomfort led me to self-medicate to the point of assured self-destruction. My genetic programming and some poor choices brought on by my environment had made me an alcoholic and prescription drug addict. Nothing was following the neat path I believed my life would follow. New York intellectuals didn't crown me as a genius, although I was not able to push for it the way some of my peers at Bard were able to. The film projects I was working on were hitting and getting stuck in roadblocks, and I was angry when my work on a book that was about to be published left only a small impression on the final outcome of the book, though a lot of the content I had reworked is contained in the pages you're leafing through.

My ego was going through gigantic changes that I had no way of measuring. I was studying Kabbalah, but only from the peripheries, watching half a lesson here and there without a group to support what I was coming to understand. I never considered shifting my point of view enough to become a committed member of a study group. The effort it required didn't make sense to me.

I only persevered through life because I knew that my work was good and I knew the screenwriting project I was working on had something to offer the world if it would ever get made, though that was a large if, and even if it did fulfill my criteria of a worthy film, I was still unsure if that was inherently valuable, though my ego definitely wanted that sort of validation. Also, even if the film was made and it was successful, it would only have a small impact on the world. I wasn't aware at the time that the internal changes I was going through would be invaluable to my spiritual growth. I wasn't yet willing to admit that the discernments I made were of any spiritual importance.

I was playing a game as I wrote, half-heartedly method acting for the sake of my ego. Sitting in an apartment, after downing bottles of liquor consistently for days, it occurred to me that even though I was in some ways moving forward with my life, it was all based on a lie I was telling myself. I was putting the best of myself forward by clouding my clarity in substances. It was the only means I knew that could clear the cobwebs. Then it was suddenly clear something needed to change. I felt like death daily. My work was sustained by prescription drugs, and these drugs, which were propelling me to push through, also gave me panic attacks on a near, nightly basis.

After living on my own for a couple of years, I was unemployed and had to move back home for a little while. Then I was kicked out of my father's house, after being let go of an easy job as a barista, making me unable to pay my rent. I was then forced into living in my mother's apartment in the East Village. She was seldom there since she lived in Long Island; I was having a grand time in the moments I wasn't paranoid or too hung over to do anything but watch television with my head stuffed into a pillow.

In spite of my apparent handicap, I got a lot done. I wrote two screenplays, was killing it in school, did a two-month editing job on a book in just two weeks, partied almost every night and acted like a rude maniac most of the time. In a state of disarray, one night, missing my phone and my wallet, I showed up at the doorstep of one of my closest friends. At Georgia's beautiful West Village apartment, I was crying about my newly ex-girlfriend and trying to sleep with the girl I had bothered at five in the morning. I repeat, I was killing it. Having gone from a neurotic to a powerhouse writer in drug-induced states of mania, I felt invincible. Still, every morning when I woke up, I felt like I needed to be hospitalized.

One night, I miraculously felt the desire to get better from this corporeal impediment, after having accumulating a bottle a day, 40-100mg a day Adderall habit (an absolutely absurd number; a man named Stephen Elliot, who I incidentally met a few times during this period, wrote a memoir about his struggles with Adderall doing 10mg/day). My friend Dave was over at my house, and I said, "I need to get sober. Will you go to an AA meeting with me?" I went that night, and I felt the familiar stench of the room—it was my third time trying to do this—and my recovery began. I began to get sober through Alcoholics Anonymous, because I felt completely out of touch with my emotional state. I allowed myself to feel the emptiness in my life for the first time in a long time, and I had opened my heart enough to consider G-d. In order to get sober, I had to look at myself from the outside and compromise my self-centered view of existence. I was a self-torturing being in the center of the universe, and I had to recognize I was only a small part of the universe and that most people didn't care about me enough to warrant my paranoia about them. It sounds so easy to let go of your belief in your control over the universe, but as you may know, lost in the grips of narcissism, the possibility never presents itself.

I was sober and beyond restless. Three substances I was heavily addicted to were expunging themselves out of my unnaturally functioning system. The headaches were intolerable. I had trouble breathing. I had forgotten how. I started to move the furniture in my mother's apartment, and sweat and chain-smoke and make tea and start to make friends in the Alcoholics Anonymous rooms with a strange, motley group of people whose happiness was infectious. They were saving their lives, just as I was saving mine. I had to go to three, sometimes four meetings a day. I tried yoga and meditation. I just needed to dull the anxiety. I was afraid of my own shadow. I shook. I was desperate and had no command of living a productive life and would do anything except for drugs to quiet the state of absolute panic. Under my psychiatrist's advice, I started taking anti-depressants, and on my own flushed the rest of my Adderall down the toilet and immediately regretted the decision. How could I work if I couldn't think coherently? The anti-depressants leveled my feelings, but I knew the joy and the sadness would be tempered. I wouldn't be living with an honest assessment of what I was feeling.

It was a strange sensation. I could see a better life after restricting something that was destroying me. Even though I had tried getting sober before, it had been two years since I considered that I might have had a problem, in spite of the fact the physical toll I experienced was far greater than it had been in the past. All I had learned two years earlier when I tried to get sober was to be a better conman. I was an alcoholic who could be thoroughly wasted and resist the desire to demean the people around me. I had made the calculation that it was too painful to do things I would regret on a regular basis, but sometimes I had lost control. I spent a morning on the street in New York searching for my wallet, the night after I arrived at my friend and writing partner's apartment, belligerently drunk and crying about my ex-girlfriend leaving me and losing any semblance of self-respect. This night and a few others made it clear I had even lost grip of the one aspect of my drinking I had any control over.

It was difficult to know that I had to exhaust myself of everything to feel real hope, and it would work as a prelude for the biggest transition of my life. AA preaches the need for G-d in your life, and as a formerly staunch atheist, I protested this and tried to work the AA program in spite of the huge obstacle it was to my recovery. If you don't turn to G-d, you can only get through the first and most important step of the program, but there are eleven more left that work to make sober life tolerable. While the program is not religious, very quickly you are told to turn your life and will over to the hands of G-d, and for the first time I felt His presence. In the deepest pits of despair, I was able to recognize a power outside of myself consciously, even after I had half-heartedly studied Kabbalah a few years earlier. The Creator, some force I couldn't imagine started to infiltrate my thoughts.

Something unknown was propelling me. While still skeptical, I was undergoing a miraculous change. After barely missing a day of drinking for two years, days and months were going by without my needing the stuff, and big external forces were pushing me to do things no one would have ever trusted me to do in the past.

Even when I had accomplished things artistically in the past, I felt spiritually deadened by them and disconnected. I couldn't appreciate my own work, since my writing was driven by the drugs shuffling through my system and inflated ego that simultaneously told me I was a genius and the lowest scum inhabiting the earth. I had given up on the idea of my own happiness at the age of twenty-five. Because of the Adderall, the legally obtained speed circulating through my blood vessels, I had cheated to accomplish it, like hitting a home run on steroids.

Subconsciously, I must have made the calculation my success wasn't real before it became a very clear blow to my ego. It was the only way I could adjust my nihilistic, or maybe even self-destructive body that didn't see the point in doing anything that wouldn't immediately gratify my senses. And besides that, I wasn't composed enough as a person to be trusted if I did truly make worthy accomplishments (completely objectively, I'm not lying when I tell you I wrote good works of literature, completely obliterated, angry and defiantly), but for what end? It wasn't getting me published, and my films weren't getting made, even as good as they were and despite how absurdly well connected I was for someone who never wholeheartedly sought or achieved full-time employment.

I came to the realization that the world doesn't revolve around me, even though that would have never occurred to me, for when you are most consumed in your ego, the thought that you spend too much time thinking about yourself doesn't exist. The world is pushed forward only by the Creator. I was an outwardly selfish person. I worried the people closest to me. Even when I was externally working hard to pull my life together, it was splitting at the seams.

I thought I was more open about the animalistic desires that beckoned me. I could get drunk and rude. I tried to sleep with a lot of women and got blackout drunk, only to take a pill the next day that could propel me just enough to get some work done, until even that worked no longer. I couldn't think with the Adderall, because my nerves had shaken me to a place where I lived in constant fear of my shadow.

I was selfish, but that was because everyone—not only me—lived a life consumed and controlled by our own capacity to receive pleasure. The only alternative is to live a spiritual life, which is something most people have no knowledge of or capacity for. My addiction was a deep yearning to be connected to a feeling of something deeper. It was a low level spiritual quest to exit myself and it had found its end.

Addicts and alcoholics are merely more open about their selfish desires than others. The sensation of drunkenness makes one feel less bad about his veiled desires, until the next day when he awakens in a state of physically and emotionally intolerable sobriety. The result of their toiling in pleasure is that they become incapable of doing what is most beneficial for them in service of a greater desire to feel OK. They want to destroy themselves with pleasure, because they can't see any benefit in making the more difficult choice of tolerating the difficulties inherent in daily life. On a low-level spiritual quest, they obsess over their feelings, unable to tolerate the state of the world, without recognizing a higher power outside of themselves. They feel good at the expense of their own life and other peoples' lives. Drugs and other people have to become their Creator, because spirituality is deadened in their vessels of reception.

Malcolm Gladwell's book, *Blink*, from a scientific point of view, explains how this disconnect occurs. He speaks with a neurologist, Antonio Damasio, about what happens mentally to drug addicted patients. Damasio says, "Addicts can articulate very well the consequences of their behavior. But they fail to act accordingly. That's because of a brain problem. That's what we were putting our finger on. Damage in the ventromedial area causes a disconnect between what you know and what you do."

The result of this is an inherent loss of intuition. Gladwell goes on to explain, "What the patients lacked was the valet silently pushing them in the right direction, adding that little emotional extra—the prickling of the palms—to make sure they did the right thing." I am still recovering from a lack of intelligent intuition. I have to address it every day at the Kabbalah lesson and in the actions I make. "In high-stakes, fast-moving situations, we don't want to be as dispassionate and purely rational as the Iowa ventromedial patients. We don't want to stand there endlessly talking through our options. Sometimes we're better off if the mind behind the locked door makes our decisions for us."[37] I could very clearly see what I was doing wrong, but I didn't have the will to enact any of the changes necessary to correct it. Every correct action felt impossible.

I was used to unearned praise. Maybe my parents loved me too much. I had given up the One True Force in the universe for petty enjoyment, and it was eating me slowly from the inside like a cancer. I wasn't making my own decisions, but a large-scale change was occurring inside of me. While I wasn't ready to resign my own ego to the will of the Kabbalah group, I was invited to a Kabbalah congress in New Jersey where I was going to be presented with an offer that would radically alter my perception of the world.

Small, Miraculous Changes

A Kabbalah congress is a conference of deeply interconnected individuals who may or may not know each other and study Kabbalah from disparate places all over the world, in order to unite. If you have done proper preparation for the congress, you are given gifts you cannot quite articulate or understand. It can be like meeting your family for the first time. Everyone reacts differently, but even to a total outsider, the happiness of the people is wholly apparent.

While it was not my first congress experience, it was the first time I could feel a deep connection with the group. It was a connection that was at once exhilarating and painful. I felt I understood the material, after having "mastered" the basics—in my small-minded ego—editing the book, but beyond that, I began to understand the importance of connection through workshops where people would work together to find answers to the questions our teacher asked.

In one of these workshops we were asked to close our eyes. It was the first time I had any real sensation of what we were achieving, and it was only a little glimpse. By closing my eyes, I could imagine our egos and the material world disappeared. Blind to the corporeality of our physical appearances, I felt I could see the universe for what it truly was—the forces propelling the material world. Our bodies slipped away, and all that was left was the light emanating from the peoples' souls. We were in one intention yearning for light from Above. It felt complete, circular, like life. Everything that our physical senses used to judge each other blew away into the ether. However, this beautiful moment passed, and a profound restlessness entered me, and given my condition, I couldn't drink it away.

I never felt such a strong weight pulling on my limbs like weights. It was as if gravity had doubled in power. I kept wondering why my father's Kabbalah mentor had asked to see me. After seven minutes on the elliptical machine, a good forty minutes less than I had been doing regularly in my early sobriety, I couldn't breathe. I didn't feel worthy of what was going to be asked of me. So I sat down and drank water for ten minutes, before I had the energy to walk to the pool in the next room. I had expected a sort of baptism to revive me from the pain.

I got into the water and swam, if you could call it that. It was closer to sinking. I could barely lift myself above the water. Back in my room I fell asleep, where my father woke me to meet with his Kabbalah teacher. I felt like nothing, stiff as a tree stump and began to think about my place in the universe, before falling asleep for an hour.

I knew I had some talent as a writer, but was unsure how these talents fit in with the goals of the group. I was also, of course, worried they had vanished with the booze and the Adderall. When I met with the teacher and a few of the main mainstays of the study group, they confirmed my belief that my work was of some relative merit. He explained how my writing was acceptable stylistically, but lacked a true understanding of the group's point of view. I needed to live in the environment of Kabbalah. I would need to have an experiential change occur; if I were to make a truly beneficial work, something would have to happen to me that I couldn't anticipate or read in a book. He didn't say any of this in so many words. He said, "You are going to write an important book. A bestseller. I don't know how long it will take. It's really up to you. It shouldn't take long, maybe six months."

Not fully invested in the group, some of the subject matter confused me to the point of disillusion. It blinded me to the purpose of Kabbalah, even after reading, writing and rewriting about the necessity of unity and connection to the Creator to the point of exhaustion. I would learn something and quickly forget it. I made statements against the group perspective in my version of the anti-Semitism book, because I believed the book had a potential to connect to people like me—people who lacked spirituality, and were unwilling to take the plunge of sacrificing something for it.

I agreed with the teacher's assessment though I was unclear why. When he asked me to move to Israel, I accepted without giving the proposition a second thought. Something above my reason gave me the strength to be willing to listen to someone pointing out a weakness of mine without any sense of malice. This had been a pattern I never had the strength to break. I would call my screenwriting professor and get into heated debates with her about what constituted a film, and I chose to ignore her sound advice that every scene needed a central tension operating upon the audience. Something in me knew that this was the only answer to all that I was lacking in my life. I shook my Kabbalah teacher's hand and agreed to take on the task, unsure of what this task was other than a book for Americans.

While it felt all too easy to accept the offer, the reality was starting to dawn on me. My body was starting to push me away from its natural path of only doing things that would clearly give me pleasure. What was I doing? What did I know about Israel? How was I going to function in the group without speaking the language? I was so different from them. Who would I make friends with? My life had been a carefully assessed struggle to remain relevant in a hip social scene in New York, though I was too cool to admit this even to myself. What would it mean if I were to leave? Even though these relationships were for the most part surface relationships, I also had close friends. Would they miss me? Would I miss them?

It wasn't like my life was perfect, but things were starting to look up in spite of the huge problems I was racking up and correcting. I was working on film scripts with promising young directors and writers. I was enrolled in graduate school, getting straight A's. I was friends with many of the hippest people of my generation, and I could play the six degrees of Kevin Bacon game to (my life in New York in a nutshell) almost every person I ever idolized or admired. Why I was stunted in an in-between place of little success and an unwillingness to push forward into a satisfying adult life, I couldn't say. I didn't know why it seemed to be happening to my entire generation across the globe. However, I was about to leave everything I knew for an opportunity to do something special.

That night I began to connect with people in ways I had never thought to do before. My ego was once both too big and too small to see any value in making connections with the group. I was talking to people about their dreams, aspirations and futures. I was making friends with people from all over the world with different backgrounds, people who had found something that gave their life true meaning. They felt something I still had no grasp of, but I was drawn to it.

I could see a light in their eyes, a clear purpose and purity in their actions. They wanted to make me comfortable, so I could participate in the connection. The celebration was big and eminent. It felt like it would never stop, but I couldn't sustain it like the others. I didn't understand or trust the ups and downs I was feeling. Was this bipolarity or the realization of everything I also thought about the world in its most honest form?

After my father went to sleep, I saw some people in the lobby of the hotel. They were commenting on the greatness this event had opened up in them.

The man I worked on the Kabbalah book with said something that stuck with me. He was thoughtful, and his smile still bleeds into my consciousness as I think of the moment. What he said may not mean much to you as a reader, but it left an indelible impression when he thoughtfully smiled, and said, "We are given some talent, some force that was endowed by the Creator. We are all working to the same goal and all given special tools to share what we have learned and connect with each other beyond the abilities we could ever achieve on our own."

He went on to list all the talents of the people in the circle. They are inconsequential as we all have something to contribute, and so he continued, "Not one of these talents is greater than any other. It is simply the gift we have been given and the tool we needed to show the world there is none else besides Him."

Just before I went to the congress, I had met the love of my life, but I was not at all ready to accept her. I was a wretch fighting her over anything I could put my finger on, blaming my beautiful Swedish girlfriend Alma, for all the discomforts I had felt in sobriety. I felt layers of issues shedding from my skin, in an angry blaze of fire. I was becoming more egotistical, less connected on a daily basis, as I tried to humble myself to my conception of G-d that was really just a wall I spoke to. I was in the most painful period of recovery from my addictions. It was a difficult period, but a purposeful suffering. I never could have opened my senses to Kabbalah when I was still convinced of my superiority to all things rooted in magic.

Still, I was thriving in school and taking anti-depressants, but I felt huge, generalized frustration and it was affecting every aspect of my life. This was all about to shatter, as I took a plunge into a country and a spiritual study I knew almost nothing about. Everything was going to fall apart before I found my way forward. Kabbalah states that our problem is that we are "in shackles," captured in the network that links us, closes us and determines all our values. We just have to dress in a certain way, eat certain food, work as prescribed, behave as accepted, and to adhere to the standard way of thinking.

We do not have our own tastes, but we have those habits that society "spoon-feeds" us. It gives us our beliefs and our actions; it affects us now through its channels, some of which can be neither recognized nor traced. We cannot block them by any protective mechanism that blocks the thoughts and desires of a large environment.

As a result, a person does not know who he is at all. After all, he is placed in the system, programmed and filled with messages that originally have no relationship with it. There is nothing you can do about it; you cannot eliminate or remove them from yourself. Even the desire to escape from these clutches is also implanted in us by this system. It turns out that I have accumulated thoughts and desires that are not mine, and I myself do not exist at all.

I had to suffer the turmoil of losing grasp of reality to find the benefit in unity and spirituality. I needed it in order to see something more majestic outside of myself.

Israel: Straight to the Creator

While I would have preferred to leave for Israel immediately following the Congress, the realities of such a life-changing move couldn't be so easy. The Creator had to put roadblocks in my path, albeit small, easy ones. Still, because of the Kabbalah group, my move was about as simple as it could be. My father clarified to me that I was a "special case," in that I would be in the group, but I didn't have to make the same sacrifice. I was given a project wherein I was at an advantage not living so closely to the path of attaining the Creator, since I would be able to better relate to the outside world. In a sense, I believed and he believed that was part of the reason I had been given this assignment. My teacher said as much when I met him, offering through a friend's translation, "Don't lose your Americaness."

The difference between a realization of spirituality and dipping my foot into it was not even a concept that occurred to me two months after the congress, when I packed up everything I owned and brought the stuff to my father's house. More accurately, l left the stuff that wasn't already there. I packed two suitcases with as much as they could possibly hold and didn't put much thought into the trip. I just left without much consideration for what I was leaving behind. I was tired of New York and needed a break, so I went to Israel for what I thought would be six months, at most a year.

It was one of my best friend's birthdays the night before I left, and I went, sober, to a bar with her and stayed up all night, too nervous to sleep before my expedition. I found myself at JFK, ready to begin my life in Israel, not at all knowing what to expect, except for the fact my father would be waiting for me at the airport in Tel Aviv. I soldiered through JFK with my huge bags and my enormous ego, ready for the flight. I was very early and already worried about the cigarettes I would not be able to smoke. It was all I thought about for the next twelve hours. I bought an e-cigarette at JFK and smoked some of it in the bathroom, and it didn't even remotely make me feel any better. I was grumpy and dissociated, thinking about my father's warnings that I needed to sleep on the plane, because there was a lot of work for us to do to settle me into my apartment when I landed.

I think the anxiety I attributed to smoking may have been masking a far greater fear. Even before I was aware of the extent of the annulment of the ego I was going to have to choose to forego if I wanted any opportunity at having a spiritual awakening, I knew I was giving up on many things. In reality, I was giving up on a sense of uncertainty. I was giving up on not having enough money to live a comfortable life in a rich city. My father, who could afford it, was happily paying for the majority of my apartment rent and bills, making this transition seamless. I was letting go of restaurant jobs and suffering. But I was also letting go of my dreams as a screenwriter. For the year I would spend there, I would be writing things that weren't the invention of my own mind. I needed a credit that would hold some merit and a substantial chance of financial success, but in doing so I would be sacrificing any chance of street cred as an atheist, Jewish intellectual who was still way too concerned with being cool and being friends with hip artists, filmmakers and models to confirm huge lacks in my own ego.

Needless to say, I couldn't sleep. This would follow me for the entirety of my first months in Israel and creep back at inopportune moments. I got off from the plane in London, ready for my connection to Tel Aviv, and was rushed to customs without an opportunity to smoke. I lit a cigarette as I got out of the transfer terminal, and a security guard yelled at me, making me cower in fear. My nicotine withdrawal gave way to an opportunity to forego thinking about anything else. I read books ten minutes at a time, before I couldn't stand to look at them any longer. All I felt was frustration, disturbing my basic ability to sit still or have a clear feeling, other than dread and confusion. I had to remind myself, "This will be worth it," tossing and turning in my seat. I had no confirmation of this fact, but I knew an interesting experience would be waiting at the other end of the flight.

It's funny that on a commercial flight, we forget how unnatural this experience is. We're like a million pound metal bird defying everything we sense about gravity. We are unburdened by what pulls us down. No one is ever more than a day or two away.

And yet, our egos only let us look at ourselves, and we focus most heavily on what we lack. For me, it was a cigarette and the comfort to fall asleep. We're soaring through the air like birds and making a journey of thousands of miles over the biggest blue ocean in the world, and all we can do is complain at the perceived lack of creature comforts to support us through a few hours that we could just as easily be at home doing the same things, watching the same movies and reading the same books.

After I got off the plane, in a daze of nicotine withdrawal and fatigue, I went to the line to get my passport stamped and then onward to enjoy my new home. I was still feeling paranoia. In my head, I was somehow convinced what I was doing was illegal, maybe morally wrong. I felt utter disdain when I was stopped by security and taken into a room for additional questioning. Barely able to speak, I walked up to the customs agent, who looked at me like a liar. His friendly face fooled me; his face covered a deeply suspicious personality who took his position as a protector of the Israeli border extremely seriously. And to be honest, I wasn't entirely sure what I was about to embark on was exactly kosher with the customs people.

I was only half-Jewish and about to spend an extended time in a country I had no affiliation with and didn't bother to apply for a special work visa or anything of that nature. So when I was stopped, maybe my worst fear had been discovered. I felt like a fake, lower than low, and my father was waiting for me. I hadn't been allowed a cigarette, and I was about to snap out of my chair, after the security people had taken my passport and left me in a room with absolutely no sense of how long I would be waiting. Like a moron, I yelled at the customs official, but somehow it seemed to work when I shouted, "This is really stressful! Why am I here? I haven't done anything wrong and someone's waiting for me!"

I was forced to wait for an hour, shaking, nervous and angry. My father called me four times, and I had no news to offer him. It was all about to change once the customs official asked a couple of disinterested questions. My leg was tapping itself. I felt like my body was consuming itself, until the relief washed over my face when he said, "Welcome to Israel." My dad was waiting as I smoked a cigarette and began to feel better, though still exhausted. We drove to my empty apartment that my father had procured for me, and I was struck by the beauty of the view, but also by the weirdness of the Israeli city. I don't quite know what I expected when I got there, but it certainly wasn't the Americanized suburb that looked like a desert version of New Jersey. The unassuming backdrop for the correction of the world felt anything but mythic and spiritual at first glance. It felt bland and American, and I felt angry about it. The intensity of my emotions immediately reified itself once I was in Israel. I felt like crying.

Everything is harder in Israel than it is in America, needlessly complicated and hot, over a hundred degrees for half of the year. Just setting up my apartment was an ordeal that I thankfully did not suffer alone. None of the appliances come in the apartment you rent, and everything is installed separately days after the appliances are delivered. The two people who need to come to install a washing machine is a metaphor for the country where people expect you are getting screwed over every time a transaction is made. People say what's on their mind instead of keeping hidden the impure intentions people have on a day-to-day basis.

While it was relatively easy to adjust to this mentality—it was exciting like a video game—, the friends, who welcomed me with open arms, was a much rougher proposition. I was still under the illusion I would be able to invest a little bit into the Kabbalah study group, work hard on my book, and relatively easily compose something beautiful. AA had taught me I needed to let go of my will to G-d, but I didn't understand what that actually meant, or if it would complement my Kabbalah study. I was told to let go of my expectations and resentments. I thought that I had, but they were always creeping back from a pit onto the surface. I wasn't upset about moving to Israel, but I did feel trapped there under my father's wallet, that I was a disappointment who needed to prove that I was spectacular, and I was going to do this on my own terms, taking the wisdom from Kabbalah and making it a palatable dessert to the secular American's life and sell millions of copies of a book with a marketable subject matter, and my once in a generation wit.

The support of the group was at first an overwhelming obstacle I couldn't understand. Everyone wanted to have me over for dinner and offered help with my transition. I thought they were overplaying the difficulty I would encounter alone in a new country, but this wasn't the case. Everything was confusing. When I met with my teacher and other people deeply involved in the group's dissemination, I didn't know what to tell them. I had been rewriting a book on anti-Semitism for months, and I wasn't quite sure what everyone was thinking about it, and it became rather clear I needed to start writing something new, but I had no idea what it would be about. It turned into the book you are holding in your hands at this moment, but I never thought I could write about myself, until after a month of going to daily Kabbalah lessons and reading vociferously. I came to the conclusion it was the only thing I was qualified to write about, and I wouldn't be writing it with my ego, the way every great writer throughout human history has worked besides the great sages.

It would stem from the Creator, the source of everything, and the results would not be easy or tangible. It would have to come from Him, because without the light of the Creator, it would be a waste of the paper it was printed on. After seeing the correct direction and knowing the correct choices, my body had a visceral, negative reaction when I decided to make these choices. The only thing that helped was going to lessons and hanging onto every word the teacher said. The only problem was that it took months to process what I was doing. Stages of complete clarity were followed by vacuous sensations of confusion and dread in relation to work. I was changing and I was happy, but I had no idea why.

A few days into my studying, I was brimming with confidence, but still, I felt a force pushing me away when I sat in the lessons. One day I would feel deeply connected (not just deeply focused) to every word coming out of my teacher's mouth. I knew his answers to questions before he had come up with them. Other times I was desperately in need of leaving my seat and feeling entirely lost. When I didn't understand the content, I was in disarray, because I couldn't rationalize or chew over what I was hearing. It felt like prison letting go of my own ego.

But as time passed, the impossible was starting to happen. I envied the friends. The lessons felt like the softest, warmest place in the world.

Finding The Collective Ego

To attain spirituality, you must remove the illusion that you have the capacity to accomplish anything without Him. You need to lose the idea your will and work ethic will accomplish what the Creator chooses to reveal through you. Every time I tried to work, I couldn't sit still long enough to write anything meaningful or personal before I was connected to the center of the group. I had to make the discernment that I needed Him.

Stuck in the mire of my ego, I was propelled by a revelation of something great that I felt integral to, but by the time I had made it to Israel I had lost all sense of purpose. The feeling I had at the congress had all but vanished. It was a distant memory.

For my spiritual growth, I needed to experience the lack that my generation felt. I needed to see that everything I had done in the past was all in the service of my ego and without it I was totally lost. Something about the lessons was revealing disconnection between what I could do with the ego and how useless it was compared to what I could do when the Creator worked through me. I needed to want connection.

About a month into my adventure, I was consumed by agony and didn't have any interest in taking in the lessons. I couldn't see how they would benefit my book. When we read from the source text of *The Zohar*, I was still trying to analyze it like literature, writing down everything the teacher said without absorbing all that much intellectually or, G-d forbid, internally. I feuded with it instead. I felt cursed by my position. The lessons were torturous and my confusion manifested itself in anxiety. I now needed the support of the group. I felt sad and alone, but my pride wouldn't allow me to ask for help. The Creator was absent, because I was not summoning Him. The world was closing in on me. I was paranoid my neighbors were talking about me in Hebrew and complaining about my smoking. I still lived in irrational fear.

The biggest obstacle was that the material was not simple for me, and everything meaningful about Kabbalah was emotional and experiential. I didn't have the strength to learn a system of Upper Worlds, being the same person who failed organismal biology in college, and I didn't have the ability to delve into something emotionally that I didn't understand.

I also had never taken the background course that offers the minimum knowledge. I only had what I retained from books and the lessons. For two months the lesson did nothing for me, but occasionally satisfy my ego when I seemed to understand something other people in the group didn't. Even when I was at odds with the lesson, I somehow felt endowed with a preternatural ability to see what was blind to others. I thought of myself as a special Kabbalist who didn't need to observe the teacher's directions fully and still be able to attain something outside of myself.

My teacher repeatedly said to my dead ears that the Creator was revealed between people. I had not made the conscious decision to live under the influence of the Light. I was a fish out of water, trying to impress others with my unmatched literary abilities, when all they wanted was my love. So I pushed with everything I had to reveal my genius thoughts. I wanted to do the job only I could do. I wanted to write a book of half-truths that would compel people to study Kabbalah. I wanted to make the study appealing to an American sensibility. I hadn't considered that this goal was utterly impossible. I could not tell people to erase themselves in a way that would appeal to anyone, especially if I didn't believe it. Something, either my morality, or the Creator wouldn't allow for it.

Slowly but surely, I was changing with very little effort. Two lessons a week and a few hours in the office was leaving imprints on my soul I was unable to comprehend. I felt I was living in a fog the first few months, because my entire perspective was shifting unconsciously. It was also quite hot, about a hundred Fahrenheit, every single day.

When we study Kabbalah, we are merely looking at the world from different colored glasses. When we live in a society that celebrates the individual, we celebrate global warming, and eventually mutually assured destruction. When we work cooperatively, the entire world can finally blossom. If we do not shift our values to communal efforts, the world is bound to destroy itself.

In "Peace in the World," an essay dating back to the early 1930s, Baal HaSulam explains that because we are all interdependent, we must apply the laws of mutual guarantee to the entire world. While the term "globalization" was not as ubiquitous in treaties of his time, his words clearly illustrate his urgent need to make the world a single, solidified unit.

"Do not be surprised if I mix together the well-being of a particular collective with the well-being of the whole world, because indeed, we have already come to such a degree that the whole world is considered one collective and one society. That is, because each person in the world draws one's life's marrow and livelihood from all the people in the world...Therefore, we can no longer speak or deal with just conducts that guarantee the well-being of one country or one nation, but only with the well-being of the whole world, because the benefit or harm of each and every person in the world depends upon and is measured by the benefit of all the people in the world."

We need to unite to correct warring powers that only work in their own self-interest, even when bodies are the cost of doing business. We must unite above the destructive ego that tells us to take everything in our path.

However, for the world to achieve mutual guarantee, it needs a role model, a group or collective that can implement unity by attaining the Creator, and by example pave the way for the rest of humankind. It is our duty to rekindle brotherly love among us. We must attain the Creator—His singular force—and pass on the method of unity to the rest of the world. We are here to bring the light of the Creator to the world, to be a light to the nations.

I needed to stupidly live in the ego of the material to understand this in my unconscious—see the utter difficulty of getting up to work in the morning without drugs, so I could truly understand the lie I had lived as a productive drug user, before becoming an unproductive one. I needed to live in these petty resentments and suffering to understand the importance of a goal that has the ability to transform our world. Kabbalah will make the world work again.

It was a struggle to gain this clarity. I had lost all ability to focus. Things that were once relatively easy for me felt impossible. I slept crazy hours, feeling consumed by a joy I never thought I could experience without a drug and the same restlessness and disconnection that those drugs would bring to me. Under the influence of drugs and my ego, I was doing my best writing. Now, I would sit at the computer for four to six hours, and nothing would come. The words that came out were random and disconnected, lacking any sense of assurance. It amounted to almost nothing usable for weeks on end. While the average worker scoffs at six hours, six hours of writing and not producing is much worse than the eight-ten hour restaurant shifts I used to do.

There is no dread like not being able to produce, feeling worthless in the only thing you are supposed to do well. Writing was my entire identity, and I was no longer functional as a writer. I had become nothing. I sensed I would have to feel great lacks to comprehend what was changing in me, but I had no idea these changes would occur so intangibly. I have heard writers say that the idea of not writing has to become less abhorrent than the difficult task of writing, but this felt like it would never end, and all I had to turn to was the lessons, and after feeling like I was wasting my time there for months, I slowly began to accumulate changes and become a different person. I used to write for my ego, and it took me a long time to write for the advancement of the group. Even as I thought I was making this change, the Creator was not allowing me to think clearly enough to express anything in a clear, cogent manner.

My memory was entirely shot. I couldn't think with any sense of clarity, and though I wrote every weekday, it was coming out in this unclear manner that had to be heavily edited to make any logical sense. In life we are conditioned to see results from the work we are doing. When we sacrifice our enjoyment for a larger goal, we see tangible results. In spirituality these results, by necessity, must be secondary to what is occurring internally.

I wanted to entertain myself endlessly, and I felt an immense desire to self destruct, blow money, sleep with women and do whatever would sabotage my work and my relationships, until a great shift occurred in my senses. Resisting these egotistical desires would end up paying dividends. I saw this decadent life was only a wasted life, but I was still a creature of bad habit, even without drugs conditioning the way I thought.

Later, in Israel, when I was fully consumed by the work of the group, the material world lost its luster for a short while, because I was a part of something above everything else. The Creator became all that mattered, and my life began to feel bigger, richer and more meaningful than I could have ever thought possible, but it would still slip out of my fingertips, because I couldn't assign value to the group properly on a consistent basis.

***

We live in a toxic society where irony reigns supreme above any genuine feelings or deep truths. We don't care about society. We don't even feel an inherent need to be part of the community we live in. We all have our own varied interests and political beliefs that work to separate us. It has gotten so bad there is no longer a common American, let alone, global experience.

Disconnect is rampant in our digital age. We can't even connect on things that used to be universal. We all listen to different music, follow different sports, read different magazines and only a fraction of us care enough to follow the news. There is no longer an educated society that votes on laws and elects representatives that look out for our best interests. We can't trust our representatives. In fact, it is assumed that our government representatives are only looking out for their own interests and the interests of the corporations that pay for their re-election. We accept this reality and live in a world of instant gratification that lets us avoid looking at the sadness that is always lurking beneath the surface. If we did not distract ourselves, we couldn't cope with the world.

When I began studying in Israel, all these things that I had a veiled awareness of were brought to the forefront of my personal reality. These perceptions were usually absent in my own life, because for about two years, part of me had grown through the ego. Even though I made very little money, I lived in a constant stream of drugs, work and distraction.

Through the reforming Light of the Kabbalah group, I began to experience reality differently. I had to be reborn, because without the drugs in my system navigating my way through the anxiety of my profession, I made myself push forward, and I physically didn't have the capacity to sit still, or concentrate, or implement a meaningful structure to my life. Once I had lost that capacity, I finally felt the juice to push me forward. As a writer I had lost all sense of fear and could let the Creator penetrate through my work. The Light could pass right through me though I had no clear course of action. My perseverance could no longer pull me through the difficult times. I had to feel everything and get in tune with my nature by feeling every aspect of life more deeply.

A Minor Revelation

What I later discerned is that I needed to share the example of my experience, because multiple books had been written about the technical aspects of Kabbalah, and they haven't brought us any closer to the correction. The material was only attainable in a group study, and it was not a necessity for spiritual growth. It was something that slowly clarifies itself to someone over a long period of time. *The Zohar* is not what I am able to share practically.

I do however have something to share. I was a completely different person then than I am today, months later, but I can't quite put my finger on how. It's not an easy thing to describe. My thoughts were completely different. I was consumed with a self-centered view of the world that had little consideration of others and wouldn't allow for me to get out of my own way.

What changed?

It was a subtle difference in the way I received knowledge that allowed me to open myself up to the study. I have become an entirely different receptor of experiences and information. The intensity of my emotions is now directed at something other

123

than my own ability to enjoy. This direction and sensation of my efforts doesn't allow for me to feel agony. I'm no longer alone. My mind and body are no longer weakened by my feelings of good and bad. I feel free from the constraints of my ego. I am softer, but not weaker, just more in tune with my environment, but also propelled by a force of strength that comes in a form of weightlessness. I feel comfortable in my own skin.

In the lessons I attend or watch on a daily basis, it has been explained on many occasions that the Light is stronger in Israel, and thus the good and bad are more apparent. The people are more emotional and closer to nature. Even as much as their country's customs and culture is Western, the place is dictated by distinct cultural differences. People are rude and proud of it. They don't see an alternative. It's like an Ayn Rand world set to techno music, where most people are kosher even though they rarely go to temple. There is nearly no evidence of the socialist, Zionist ideal that the country was built upon outside the remaining kibbutzim.

I had no idea how intense the feelings would become in the lessons, but in order to achieve heaven in this life, you have to feel the lowest pits of despair. I always intuitively understood this reality and always fought against it with the will of an egotist. I wrote about this concept constantly, usually about matters of the heart or drug consumption. The sweet is only sweet when it is compared to the sour. Like Adam, when he was biting into the tree of knowledge, the whole of sin would rush upon me in due time. I would feel the wrath of my own ego.

Back then, I was making myself miserable, but the glimmer of hope that my girlfriend could come and open me up to new experiences in the odd country I had chosen to move to gave me some hope. It didn't prevent me from yelling at my father on the phone and blaming him for my inability to adapt to the world that had become a part of him. I was playing a game of tightrope with the group. In spite of my belief that I needed to build a life in Tel Aviv with people more similar to me, instead of considering there was something for me in the group, the group became the source of pleasure that I would reject in favor of my rational mind.

After a few weeks of slowly integrating myself into the group, I made the decision to hold off on exploring Israel until my girlfriend, Alma, came to visit me. What began with the best of expectations had turned into the most difficult passage of time in my entire life. About two months into my journey to Israel the unthinkable happened, and what I chose to do after the frightful day was indirectly reject the group, and the pain just seeped further to the edge of my consciousness. I wasn't angry with the Creator, I just saw Him as absent.

I hadn't seen Alma for a few weeks before I came, because she had moved back to Sweden. We Skyped on a daily basis and stayed close to each other, and I began to cherish her, appreciate her more than I ever had before in my egotistical specter. I saw her as a lifeline, the thing that would be able to give me strength as I started to annul my very large ego to the work in Israel. When I got there, I wasn't aware of what annulment meant, and I was absolutely unwilling to do a thing that would diminish my intellectual growth. I saw this assignment as an opportunity to learn the basics about the group and offer them as a rational explanation of the science of Kabbalah, that if I could debate the validity of what we were doing somehow, I could convert those who opposed Kabbalah into supporters. I still believed it was valuable to study Kabbalah in the wrong direction. I thought I could offer Kabbalah as something that added to your life, that if you could establish a contact with G-d, you would see Kabbalah as an efficient means to take this plunge as an irrational push towards a better life. I didn't quite understand that faith above reason was a rational means of attaining spirituality.

I was coarse by nature, and if I hadn't been placed into the center of the Kabbalah group, I never would have benefited from it. I didn't really have the constitution, or the desire. My spiritual yearning was covered in layers of nonsense. I resisted connection, because I still highly believed in the values my upper class, liberal American values had taught me. I hated to give up my own knowledge in favor of a system. Unlike many others in the group, I felt like by submitting to Kabbalah studies, I was letting go of things that were invaluable to me. I still loved parts of my ego.

I had started to work at home, because I found working in the factory to be distracting and debilitating. I slept during the days and stayed awake all night to watch the lesson. I did whatever was necessary to be connected from the source of wisdom, while I was disconnected from the group on a personal level. I looked at the people before me like fools for rejecting their own intellect for this wisdom and not using it as an additional system of information like I had been doing. These feelings kept popping up, over and over again, relentlessly.

Then Alma came and I was able to explore Israel. I needed a break from the intensity of Kabbalah study just as I was beginning to believe in it fully and fight it all at once. Even in my disconnection, the light of the group was altering my perception. I began to feel something. I wanted to connect with the Creator, and without tangible connection with others, I was getting glimpses of illuminations just by studying content I didn't really understand.

In the lessons I was feeling buzzing in my soul. It was a warm, womb-like feeling. The Creator was penetrating my body, confirming the words of the teacher had power by giving me little glimpses of spiritual connection. In these moments, the entire purpose of existence was clear to me for the first time, but unrealized. I had found something better than anything I had ever felt.

Still, with this feeling, my mind would return to its old ways, and I ran away from these life-affirming feelings, because my pride wouldn't allow me to let go of all the efforts I had made for corporeal benefit. I still felt I could find something more meaningful on my own, and forces from above that were handed to me like prescient little gifts were not enough to make me reconfigure my life towards spiritual yearning.

With Alma by my side, I continued to skeptically attend the lessons, encouraging her to go with me to Shabbat meals, where the group would eat together. Men and women attended the lesson on Saturday together, and the group became a real community. The warmth was infectious. Everyone treated each other like they were best friends with huge smiles on their faces.

I was consumed by this feeling, but I couldn't stop thinking about Alma's brother, who had been missing for a few days. It was a damper on my enthusiasm, and though Alma and I were having an amazing time in the group and exploring Tel Aviv, before our little trip I had planned to Tiberias and Tzfat, I could sense that this moment was going to end badly. The tension between good and miserable was palpable. Alma also felt a connection with the group. For her it was much easier. She wasn't half as bitter as me.

I took a few days off writing to go on a little trip, farther north in Israel to "holy" places. These places, in spite of their historical import, held no power. I found myself missing the group. I felt out of touch with existence. I needed support Alma and I, in spite of our love, did not know how to offer one another. We were weakened by the toll of not knowing where Alma's brother was and a lack of spiritual connection. Though we had fun, something was lacking, and we were feeling exhausted and withdrawn. We walked through the graveyard in Tiberias, trying to feel some sort of connection with the Israeli people. Wild horses roamed through the mountains. We swam like Jesus in the Sea of Galilee. We looked at the mountains and felt our smallness.

In Tzfat, we walked until our limbs could move no longer. On the bus ride back, we passed out from exhaustion after seeing the tomb of the ARI and walking through the old cobblestone city. I imagined the journeys Kabbalists had to take up huge hills in relative isolation to a city on a hill where men had tirelessly used *The Zohar* to attain the Creator. But I did not feel the aura of the place, the way I felt it on a daily basis in the lesson. I had just then come to understand that the Creator does not exist in holy places, but inside our connection with one another.

The next day I went to work, and when I went back at lunchtime to pick up a book, Alma was on the phone with her mother. What I had suspected, but did not want to believe or say out loud, had happened.

Alma's brother was dead. The initial shock was harrowing and I had never felt so sad for another person. I made the arrangements for Alma to go back and lived in a haunted sense of terror that couldn't have been a fraction of what she felt. I decided to go to visit my father at his home in Italy and then visit Alma to be with her in her time of need.

I didn't want to change myself, even though I knew it was in service of something far greater than I could ever hope to achieve alone. I felt the shame of losing my keys, not creating at the level that had been expected of me and sat on the peripheries of my girlfriend's brother's death, not knowing the victim, but seeing how it affected Alma. I still listened to the lessons and was angry at the group and at the Creator for the situation I was in, how much His absence had hurt someone so full of life and so deeply loved.

Discernments

I came back from a tragedy in Sweden with a chip on my shoulder. I felt I needed the group to support me, but I didn't want to need anyone. As I listened to my teacher speak about young people—how they felt no power to do anything or create anything meaningful—I felt he was wrong about much, and I resented his characterization of an entire segment of the population. I understood that everyone had to deal with these tragedies, that the state of our world was destructive and that death was inevitable. It didn't matter. In my state of sadness, I returned to my ego. It was what I knew best and I got lost in an internal fight with what the teacher was saying about people in general that I took as a personal attack.

And it was absolutely true that I knew intelligent and motivated people. And it was clear that I had been extremely motivated for sections of my life, but that motivation was at the expense of others well-being and my own, and that motivation was largely fake and drug fueled. And people who had interest in scientific discovery and cultural achievements were an exception to the trajectory of society, certainly not the norm. These people were still on a forward trajectory as the rest of the world waited in the wings, slowly and carelessly becoming negative forces on the health of their societies by taking and offering nothing in return. When they looked inwardly outside the pure intention of their work, it was done for the selfish desire of appearing greater than their fellow men. These egos all working for their own self-interests and the systems that contain them creates a world, in perpetually, expanding states of crisis. When we see all our assumptions about society as a means to protect us, it collapses like a demolished building. The foundations are crumbling, and if we refuse to unite, these warning signs will become full-fledged disasters on the scale of the Holocaust. Only we won't be able to come out of them.

Like society, I needed to build a new foundation over a demolished building. I was exhausted, annoyed and hungry, as the hot wind bristled through my hair. I walked up the stairs of the study center in a daze to see hundreds of people. I found a few friends in the hordes of people who were chain-smoking in preparation for the day of fasting. As a Reform Jew and secular humanist, I had never fasted for the entire day. In all honesty, I didn't think I could go through with the ritual. I was never much for rituals.

We all went inside and I put my headphones on to listen to the prayers for the meal and the wisdom to be imparted upon my ears. I was ready for a beautiful piece of filet mignon, and out came soggy, tasteless chicken soup that I gulped down with a plastic spoon and was sure to take seconds, just in case I was still to go through with the fast.

I walked home after the meal annoyed by everything that had just gone on. There were no cars on the street. Everything was quiet. I missed the loud noises and crowds of New York. I felt like the last man on earth. I went to sleep and woke up grumpy for the next lesson, an hour late. I felt guilty that a new year started off so lazily. I went to the lesson, sat through it pensively and ran home to go back to sleep, in order to stop feeling this dread. I slept for a while, went back to the study center for the final prayers, and I watched them like a ticking time bomb, waiting to put food in my stomach.

As the days passed, I stubbornly kept at the study. I felt an opportunity to start fresh. Except sleeping in a few times, I didn't miss anything for the remainder of the week, and this sense of dread diminished. The group became a cure for the grief. It healed everything. When I did little actions of impure bestowal, as simple as helping stack chairs, I felt a part of something larger. When I told people about what had happened, they offered their help, but the gestures weren't empty. They felt my sadness, and by filling my lack, we were inalterably connected to one another. What I didn't understand or had forgotten was that our lacks and the fulfillment of them was the very action pushing us towards the spiritual world.

Then this absent perception of reality became clear. I noticed everyone sleeping on the high holidays was a symptom of our connection; the group has the power to make people live in the same desire. I began to admire the dedication of the friends. Since it was the holy holidays, I made the decision to attend the majority of the meals and lessons, even though I didn't really want to. Just by making this step, I blended in with and became clothed by the group. They took care of me through my troubles. I saw the New Year as an opportunity to correct what I had lacked before. It gave me an opportunity to work.

Though the book was still a huge obstacle I wasn't tackling well, I became a part of the study group without any reservations. I began to see myself as a student of my teacher instead of as something separate. Though this period was not easy, the warmth of the group made it tolerable and gave me preparation for actually seeing the Creator in the group and working through bestowal. Of course my ego blocked me from living this way permanently, but I was tied into the direction of the group. I cared for them as they cared for me.

Strange Circumstances

We are all victims of circumstances that we are forced to transcend without the ability to. When we look at the popular films of our era, we see people enslaved in horrific situations, before being able to overcome impossibly harsh situations to survive and save the world. This confirms the collective consciousness of the world right now that is still in the early stages of the speaking level of development. Our egos feel enslaved, but are cathartically able to fantasize about overcoming this reality, while still existing in self-imposed enslavement to our desires. In the words of the mad-genius rapper, Kanye West, in his interview on the radio station Power 105.1, where he controversially expresses a desire to be from a wealthy Jewish family, he shows us that no matter what we're able to accomplish materially, these efforts are going to only create larger frustrations.

"I really wanted to express as a modern-day poet...The most relevant is to be a rap-rockstar... We're not each other's enemies. I'm showing y'all how we work together. But in fashion or product design they try and marginalize us and say that we can only have an urban clothing line or we can only do this. And of course we gonna have a clothing line, we gonna wear it to death and then it's gone...It ain't that I feel like a slave. We are mentally enslaved. We enslaved to brands, we enslaved to a Benz symbol, we enslaved to chains, a woman is enslaved to the concept a diamond are a girl's best friend. Girls in London don't even wear engagement rings. That's all been programmed into us. When we born, we born artists, we born free and we're held down by society's perception of us. We just don't wanna be embarrassed...You need product. You need to own something to have a voice in this world...When you have money, ain't nobody can fire you."[38]

Even Kanye West, who has achieved so much—21 Grammys and millions of dollars in the bank—feels restricted by the powers that be, has a desire to connect, but it is swallowed by his desire to have more money than anyone else, so he can dominate others. He sees the extent of how society programs the way we think and the necessity of working together to improve the world, but without the Creator, he believes this can be done by material means. His intelligence and ego make him feel entitled to change the world and he may be a better leader than most people give him credit for, but his vision misses the one essential piece, the Upper World. We cannot all become billionaires and control the output of information, but there are alternatives. Kanye doesn't realize that if his tens of millions became billions, he would still be burdened by the same desire for more and be as powerless as he feels now. If he had a larger influence on the world it may be more aesthetically beautiful, but it wouldn't do anything to change the way we all feel.

What do we get out of this?

The only correction to the world will come from a spiritual source and this material excess will be worth nothing. Though Kanye and other people fueled by their egos will argue this point by citing the importance of Steve Jobs, fashion designers, artists and intellectuals, there are no longer any great sages in our society. The great people are limited by the material world. While their accomplishments are incredible, they are bound by the world we can see, while infinity (*ein sof*) awaits us.

Sages, like The ARI and Baal HaSulam had unprecedented knowledge and desire to reshape the universe directly from the Creator. Since we are not men of this nature, we need to develop new senses through our Kabbalah studies on a daily basis. Nothing else has the power to alter us from our slavery to our lowly desires. All the money in the world won't fight existential dread when the world suffers.

In order to transcend our self-victimization, we have to stop looking at what the Creator gives us as good or bad. It simply is. We must accept what is put in front of us, except for our lack of connection with the Creator. We need work only for the purpose of attaining a real life in the spiritual world above the ego. Our imagined enslavement must be reconsidered as propulsion given to us from Above to find meaning that the ego has shattered from our consciousness.

Our perceived concept of pleasure is an illusion that holds us back from real pleasure. This is only achieved through mutual guarantee, which is an entire reversal of our nature as humans. We have the capacity to be G-d-like, and even in the context of the center of the group we can blind ourselves to this fact. While blows can push us to propel from below upwards, it is only an initial step, before the light that reforms guides us to correct our nature and see that the only thing that benefits us is giving pleasure to the Creator. He leads us to Him with small illuminations until we achieve this purpose.

If you choose to divert yourself from truth, you can be hurt by the disappointments of your life that led you here, but it is not our job to philosophize over the Creator's intention. It is our job to let the Creator work through us, by submitting our ego to His illuminations. The greatest and only true force in the universe is accessible and because of the culture of endless entertainment with little effort we don't want it.

But we can turn to Him. We do this together in a group. When someone prays alone, one is limited by his or her own ego. They wish to satiate their own desires, even if their desires are for the benefit of someone else. For this reason, it is impossible to achieve spirituality by this means. Praying in one intention is what Kabbalists call "the prayer of many." We pray together in a group, because it shields us from the inevitable suffering that will come in our lives when we care for ourselves above others and above the Creator.

In a group, we can learn the true meaning of life and no longer separate the good or the bad in any given situation. If you experience a great tragedy, it feels impossible for your ego not to be angry at the Source. If you see the Creator as everything, you will direct your anger to him. You will feel lost and push away any possibility of a solution, unless you are under the influence of the light and the correct environment.

In a group, you are able to achieve something called complete love. When this intention occurs in a man, he is able to rise above what he feels. He understands that suffering does not mean the Creator is bad. This suffering only propels him to clear his vessels to feel a stronger connection with the Creator, to feel the pure love of G-d that can transcend the meaning of life.

This was so true to every path of correction. After months of bliss, since Yom Kippur, I went to visit my father essence of my being, but then I started to doubt the Creator and veer away from the in Italy for a Christmas break. My mother and brother were there and after Italy, they came to visit me in Israel with Alma. We had a wonderful time, exhaustively traveling to Tel Aviv, Jerusalem and The Dead Sea in three days. My disconnection wasn't the result of anything I did, but what I didn't allow myself to do.

Maybe it was just the happy passage of time without the group, but I lacked any sense of urgency and began going to lessons without any real regularity and losing touch with what was important. I wasn't challenging myself to connect with others. I was returning to living only for my enjoyment. I barely looked at my book and had little to no communication with my friends. I lost all sense of urgency and began to doubt I was doing anything of import. Falling back into old patterns, I went from agreeable and happy to restless.

I felt myself holding onto small pleasures. I was wrapped up in nonsense, wishing I could push forward with the book, while I waited for the Creator to get me out of an abyss I had created for myself. I had lost touch with what I had learned in Kabbalah, not so much any knowledge, but something intangible that was dependent on my new vessels that gave me the ability to love others, free from fear and embarrassment. I only thought of myself, but I did not love this person consuming all my thoughts, until all of a sudden, I felt the ability to love and care for the group and every being on this earth.

One day, alone, after everyone had left, and I began making efforts to re-acclimate myself to the group (going to lessons with a little cold), late one night before the lesson, the earth sounded like it was shaking. Thunder struck. With the wind whooshing through the air outside my apartment, everything was suddenly clear. I understood that I had begun to see the group the way the rest of the world assesses each other, like strangers. I needed to overcome this impediment and the power I needed would come from Him. Though I had the illumination, my body was physically sick with a stomach flu that wouldn't exit my body.

I recalled one of the books I read over my Christmas vacation. In Chuck Klosterman's pop culture investigation of evil, *I Wear the Black Hat*, he considers the people he comes into contact with on a daily basis, the thousands of Brooklynite strangers he sees but rarely acknowledges.

He begins his book, "I certainly don't dislike them, because I have no reason to do so. If one of these strangers were suddenly in trouble and I had the ability to help, I absolutely would – but I suspect my motive for doing so might not be related to them. I think it would be the result of all the social obligations I've been ingrained to accept, or perhaps to protect my own self-identity, or maybe because I'd feel like a coward if I didn't help a damaged person in public (or maybe because others might see me actively ignoring a person in need). I care about strangers when they're abstractions, but I feel almost nothing when they're literally in front of me."[39]

Most of us have absolutely no feelings for the strangers outside of our windows. If we really looked deeply at our thoughts about them, we'd clearly see that they mean almost nothing to us, and it would seem unreasonable if they did. We believe they have no connection to us, and they don't, in any direct way. It is, however, difficult to come to this conclusion, because it forces us to admit our lack of moral strength.

People avoid being honest about their own feelings, and thus are burdened by a shame that blocks them from opening their hearts to others as Nature intended. In spirituality we erase this shame. All our shame is processed by our connection, or lack thereof, in relation to the Creator. As I've previously noted, the Light cures everything. This isn't some unproven theory, as I have seen it happen with my own eyes.

Sick in bed, I was living in shame that was blocking me from working, and more importantly, connecting and depending on the group. I wasn't getting better, and my mind was working against me. I knew how to make the correction, but my body blocked me from this. I'm intolerable to be around when I'm sick, so I try and keep to myself. I was alone. Stuck in bed, unable to get out of bed for six days over the course of two weeks. I felt paranoia about an infection destroying my body.

Determined to start working at the center on a regular basis instead of toiling alone at home without the force of the Light, the Creator was making this task more difficult. I was in a pattern of finding bodily and mental excuses and trying to write with some clarity from time to time, but nothing was stable. I felt I didn't have the strength to write the book on my own. I was left recalling and salivating over the times I could use ADHD medicine to focus intently for hours on end. I was literally willing to destroy my body and with it any sense of emotional wellbeing, just to not be stuck in this feeling of literary incompetence. I would do anything to feel a sense of control, because I was spiritually constipated. I was not willing to leave room in my thoughts for the Creator.

***

It was the end of January. I made myself a deadline of March 15th and found myself in an emotional tug of war before the congress. I wanted to allow myself to love with the same enthusiasm I saw from the people who came to Israel for this greater unified purpose, but a part of me was holding back. I felt huge obstacles preventing me from opening my heart to the path of the Creator, both real and invented.

A week before the thunder struck life into me in my flu state, my girlfriend, Alma, was sick in my bed, teeth clattering, unresponsive and shaking. She tried to breathe, but all she could manage was to vibrate like a dryer. We had just left dinner early on account of her pain. She could barely stand straight, but as she was given to fits of dizziness, I thought little of it. The night before, she had woken me up with her pain, and I told her to go to sleep. She was a bit of a dramatist and a hypochondriac, so I assumed it couldn't be as serious as it looked.

I was helpless asking her to relay her symptoms and went so far as to call the ambulance before she waved to signal me to stop. Finally, after fifteen minutes of watching the poor girl in turmoil, she collected herself and I dragged her to the hospital down the street for the second time. How I dreaded that place from the last time I was there. Luckily, there was little in the way of drama after her legs shook too much for her to walk twenty feet from the doctor's desk to the dingy, aqua green-blanketed hospital bed. I was frightened at my core. I stood nervously, looking down at my beautiful girlfriend in visible pain, unaware I could grab a plastic chair to rest on.

It was the most helpless feeling, seeing someone you love in trouble with no control over the outcome. It recalled the feeling I had when her brother died. She had a kidney infection, like her mother suspected, and she got an IV, and we sat together for a very long time. We sat nervously through the night into the morning, past the Shabbat lesson, I had promised a great friend I would be attending. I knew it was in the hands of the Creator, just as my sickness was creating an obstacle for me to tune myself into an environment of bestowal.

***

A few weeks later, after Alma had gone home, I too had to see a doctor, though it wasn't nearly as dramatic. The kind Dr. Jonas told me I was fine, that it was absurd to believe my girlfriend transmitted a kidney infection and prescribed rest. I got better, before getting worse. The night before a trip to a congress in southern Israel, I called the doctor, saying I had the most awful, blinding headache in my life, that my bones were sore. I felt sharp pains in my heart and my stomach was growling. He insisted nothing was wrong with me and the virus had come back and that rest would be needed. I assumed I would skip the trip to the desert, because Dr. Jonas regretfully said as much. But after rationalizing there was so much more Congress for me to take in later in the week, something jolted me out of bed. I needed to fight through the cold, because I didn't know when else would I ever go to the desert and sleep in tents with my friends. Though I was in a state of doubting my role in Israel and the importance of our work, I still cared for my friends and didn't want to disappoint them. Waiting for the bus at dawn, I felt uncomfortable. I looked for familiar faces, but didn't have enough energy or confidence to say *shalom* to anyone.

Clearly, the beauty of the desert was in itself an awe-inspiring sight that drew the group into a feeling of smallness, but natural beauty had nothing to do with the spirituality we were about to enter. The entire group had to prepare a tent with electrical wiring to broadcast events and lessons. The chairs had to be set up just so. We had to make our own food. We had to work for the purpose of each other with the intention to bestow to the Creator.

Separated from the outside world, the group was living in a state as close to pure bestowal as human beings were capable of. There were no egos in sight. At the very least, they were hidden.

We all felt responsible for one another. Thousands had made the journey from abroad to connect with one another in a singleness of purpose to attain the Creator. The Congress was in many ways like the ones I had attended before; people played music, listened to lessons, raised toasts, danced and spoke to people they had only seen before on television screens, but something was different. Something transcendent was happening.

Consumed by the power of bestowal, I felt the urgency of connecting with and helping the friends. Even on the bus ride, I was beginning to connect with people like I never had before. My sickness was no longer. I began to clearly see that the natural order of the universe was built in connection, that our self-awareness had created a sense of destructive self-interest that can only be cured in effort for one another above the individual selves. Everyone sensed something big was changing. Everyone felt compelled to tell each other that they loved the other. Everyone made thousands of discernments in the workshops, and we were no longer only observers; we were participating in the prophecy of bestowal. We were compelling each other to be better by example, even if we couldn't speak the same language. We felt the power of the Universe at our feet. I had never felt such pure ecstasy as when I sat in the lesson under a tent, when I helped set up mats for us to sleep on and had talks with other people working in service of the other to attain the Higher Source. We had broken past the raspberry sphere. It was a glimpse of infinity (*ein sof*).

This seemingly contrary action has made the unknowable possible. Sacrificing my ego has made me fully formed. When I got here, I was doing everything in my power to prevent this from happening, though I didn't know it at the time. I stopped being consumed with myself by directing my thoughts and prayers to others, working against my nature to get the group and the world closer to perfection.

144

While I am by no means perfect and cannot claim to live in a state of constant attainment or even serenity, or nirvana, something untraceable about my perception of the world was altered. I attained nothing tangible, but what now lives in me is an ideal to turn to and build upon. It is a clear meaning of existence that I found accidentally. I react to the world differently and began to love the group, truly love people for the first time in years. These people who were once separate entities were a part of my soul.

For two days in the desert, the shattering of the vessel that Adam instigated seemed like a distant memory—a remnant of a past world where egos feuded with each other. We could feel each other the same way we feel ourselves in our own sensations and it propelled us to glimpse the power of the Creator. We felt the sensation of home, and for many of us for the first time. We were a part of nature, and, though the feeling is impossible to describe, it confirmed everything I had ever doubted about the study was of little importance, that if we could sustain the power of mutually beneficial actions outside our group, we could transform the world. There'd be a tectonic shift. It felt like an answer to a question we never knew how to ask.

Notes

1.   Mark Harris, "Twilight of the Tummelers," New York Magazine (May 24th, 2009), http://nymag.com/movies/features/56930/

2.   ibid

3.   Hitchens, Christopher. *G-d is Not Great: How Religion Poisons Everything*. New York: Twelve, 2007.

4.   Jordan Belfort, *The Wolf of Wall Street*, Random House Publishing Group, 2007

5.   Ayn Rand, "Textbook of Americanism," 84, The Ayn Rand Column, http://aynrandlexicon.com/lexicon/individualism.html

6.   *The Talented Mr. Ripley*, Anthony Minghella, Miramax, 1999, Film.

7.   "Nikola Tesla"; by Nikola Tesla as told to George Sylvester Viereck (February 1937). http://www.pbs.org/tesla/res/res_art11.html. PBS.org.

8.   Gladwell, Malcolm. *Blink: The Power Of Thinking Without Thinking*. New York : Little, Brown And Co., 2005

9.   Gary Shteyngart, *Absurdistan*, United States: Random House, 2006.

10.   Tina Fey and Jack Burditt. *30 Rock/The Fighting Irish*. NBC. 8 Mar. 2007. Television.

11.   Chopra, Deepak. *How to Know G-d: The Soul's Journey into the Mystery of Mysteries*. New York: Crown, 2000. Print.

12.   Smith, Robert Holbrook, and Bill W. *The Big Book of Alcoholics Anonymous: The Story of How Many Thousands of Men and Women Have Recovered from Alcoholism*. United States: Lark, 2013. Print.

13.   "Elisabeth Sahtouris: Holistic Biology (excerpt) -- A Thinking Allowed DVD W/ Jeffrey Mishlove." YouTube. YouTube, 31 Aug. 2010. Web. 13 May 2014.

14.   Johnson, Steven. *Emergence: The Connected Lives of Ants*, Brains, Cities, and Software. New York: Scribner, 2001. Print.

15.   ibid

16.   Hitchens, Christopher. *G-d is Not Great: How Religion Poisons Everything.* New York: Twelve, 2007.

17.   By Israel we mean what was once Jews and now is people with a point in a heart from every nation. The nation of Israel is a spiritual connection with the Creator by a united people, not the country.

18.   *Masechet Yoma,* p 9b.

19.   Rav Moshe Ben Maimon (Maimonides), *Mishneh Torah* (*Yad HaChazakah* (The
20.   Mighty Hand), Part 1, "The Book of Science," Chapter 1, Item 3.

 Rabbi Shmuel Bornstein, *Shem MiShmuel* [*A Name Out of Samuel*], *Haazinu* [Give Ear], TARAP (1920).

21.   Rav Yitzhak HaCohen Kook (the Raiah), *Letters the Raiah* vol. 2, 34

22.   Odenheimer, Micha (December 16, 2004). "Latter-day luminary". *Haaretz.*

23.   Rabbi Isaiah HaLevi Horowitz (The Holy Shlah), In *Ten Utterances*, "Sixth Utterance."

24.   Rabbi Shimon Ashkenazi, *Yalkut Shimoni* [The Shimoni Anthology], Micah, Chapter 7, continuation of intimation no. 556.

25.   Rabbi Isaiah HaLevi Horowitz (The Holy Shlah), "Gate of Letters," Item 60, "Satisfaction."

26.   Fitzgerald, F. Scott. *The Great Gatsby*, New York: Charles Scribner's Sons, 1925.

27.   ibid

28.   Clive Thompson, "Are Your Friends Making You Fat?", *The New York Times* (September 10, 2009), http://www.nytimes.com/2009/09/13/magazine/13contagion-t. html?_r=1&th&emc=th

29.   Christian Jarrett, Ph.D, "Mirror Neurons: The Most Hyped Concept in Neuroscience?" Psychology Today (December 10, 2012), url: http://www.psychologytoday.com/blog/brain-myths/201212/mirror-neurons-the-most-hyped-concept-in-neuroscience

30.   ibid.

31.   Nicholas A. Christakis, James H. Fowler, *Connected: The Surprising Power of Our Social Networks and How They Shape Our Lives -- How Your Friends' Friends' Friends Affect Everything You Feel, Think, and Do* (USA, Little, Brown and Company, January 12, 2011), 305.

32.   Rav Yehuda Leib HaLevi Ashlag (Baal HaSulam), *The Writings of Baal Ha-Sulam*, "The Freedom" (Israel: Ashlag Research Institute, 2009), 414.

33.   Rav Yehuda Leib HaLevi Ashlag (Baal HaSulam), *The Writings of Baal Ha-Sulam*, "The Freedom," 419.

34.   ibid.

35.   John Cloud, "Why Your DNA Isn't Your Destiny," Time Magazine (January 06, 2010), url: http://www.time.com/time/magazine/article/0,9171,1952313,00.html.

36.   ibid.

37.   Gladwell, Malcolm. *Blink: The Power Of Thinking Without Thinking*. New York : Little, Brown And Co., 2005.

38.   "Kanye West Interview." Power 105.1 FM. N.p., n.d. Web. 13 May 2014. <http://www.power1051fm.com/media/podcast-breakast-club-interviews-breakfastclub_interviews/kanye-west-interview-24021364/>.

39.   Klosterman, Chuck. *I Wear the Black Hat: Grappling With Villains* (Real and Imagined). N.p.: Scribner, 2013. Print.

Further Reading

To help you determine which book you would like to read next, we have divided the books into six categories— Beginners, Intermediate, Advanced, Good for All, Textbooks, and For Children. The first three categories are divided by the level of prior knowledge readers are required to have in order to easily relate to the book. The fourth category, Good for All, includes books you can always enjoy, whether you are a complete novice or well versed in Kabbalah.

The fifth category, Textbooks, includes translations of authentic source materials from earlier Kabbalists, such as the Ari, Rav Yehuda Ashlag (Baal HaSulam) and his son and successor, Rav Baruch Ashlag (the Rabash). The category, For Children, includes books that are suitable for children ages 3 and above. Those are not Kabbalah books per se, but are rather inspired by the teaching and convey the Kabbalistic message of love and unity.

Additional material can be found at www.kabbalah.info. All materials on this site, including e-versions of published books, can be downloaded free of charge.

BEGINNERS

A Glimpse of Light: The Basics of the Wisdom of Kabbalah

A Glimpse of Light: The Basics of the Wisdom of Kabbalah offers selected contemplations from the ocean of wisdom contained in the wisdom of Kabbalah. This book touches upon topics such as pleasure, ego, love, men and women, globalization, education, ecology, Nature, perception of reality, *The Book of Zohar*, and spirituality. Just open the book wherever you wish, and begin to read. Each chapter contains several sections that combine to form a complete picture. This collection will serve you as a "glimpse of the Light," a window into the profound emotions and perceptions we can all attain by studying the wisdom of Kabbalah.

The Spiritual Roots of the Holy Land

The Spiritual Roots of the Holy Land takes you on a wondrous journey through the land of Israel. As you take in the breathtaking pictures of the holy land, another layer of the age-old country is revealed—its spiritual roots, the ebb and flow of forces that have shaped the curvy landscape that is sacred to billions of people around the world. At the end of the book, you'll find roadmaps of Israel, to help you locate each place you visit, whether in mind or in body, and more details on the forefathers who have made this land the focal point of an entire planet.

Self-Interest vs. Altruism in the Global Era: How society can turn self-interests into mutual benefit

Self-Interest vs. Altruism in the Global Era presents a new perspective on the world's challenges, regarding them as necessary consequences of humanity's growing egotism, rather than a series of errors. In that spirit, the book suggests ways to *use* our egos for society's benefit, rather than trying to suppress them.

...Stating that society's future relies on cooperation of people to work together for society, stating that much of society's degradation in recent decades has been the result of narcissism and greed, *Self Interest vs. Altruism* is a curious and recommended read.

James A. Cox, Editor-in-Chief, *Midwest Book Review*

A Guide to the Hidden Wisdom of Kabbalah

A Guide to the Hidden Wisdom of Kabbalah is a light and reader-friendly guide to beginners in Kabbalah, covering everything from the history of Kabbalah to how this wisdom can help resolve the world crisis.

The book is set up in three parts: Part 1 covers the history, facts, and fallacies about Kabbalah, and introduces its key concepts. Part 2 tells you all about the spiritual worlds and other neat stuff like the meaning of letters and the power of music. Part 3 covers the implementation of Kabbalah at a time of world crisis.

Kabbalah Revealed: A Guide to a More Peaceful Life

This is the most clearly written, reader-friendly guide to making sense of the surrounding world. Each of its six chapters focuses on a different aspect of the wisdom of Kabbalah, illuminating its teachings and explaining them using various examples from our day-to-day lives.

The first three chapters in *Kabbalah Revealed* explain why the world is in a state of crisis, how our growing desires promote progress as well as alienation, and why the biggest deterrent to achieving positive change is rooted in our own spirits. Chapters Four through Six offer a prescription for positive change. In these chapters, we learn how we can use our spirits to build a personally peaceful life in harmony with all of Creation.

Wondrous Wisdom

This book offers an initial course on Kabbalah. Like all the books presented here, *Wondrous Wisdom* is based solely on authentic teachings passed down from Kabbalist teacher to student over thousands of years. At the heart of the book is a sequence of lessons revealing the nature of Kabbalah's wisdom and explaining how to attain it. For every person questioning "Who am I really?" and "Why am I on this planet?" this book is a must.

Awakening to Kabbalah: The Guiding Light of Spiritual Fulfillment

A distinctive, personal, and awe-filled introduction to an ancient wisdom tradition. In this book, Rav Laitman offers a deeper understanding of the fundamental teachings of Kabbalah, and how you can use its wisdom to clarify your relationship with others and the world around you.

Using language both scientific and poetic, he probes the most profound questions of spirituality and existence. This provocative, unique guide will inspire and invigorate you to see beyond the world as it is and the limitations of your everyday life, become closer to the Creator, and reach new depths of the soul.

Kabbalah, Science, and the Meaning of Life

Science explains the mechanisms that sustain life; Kabbalah explains why life exists. *Kabbalah, Science, and the Meaning of Life* combines science and spirituality in a captivating dialogue that reveals life's meaning.

For centuries, Kabbalists have been writing that the world is a single entity divided into separate beings. Today the cutting-edge science of quantum physics states a very similar idea: that at the most fundamental level of matter, we are all literally one.

Science proves that reality is affected by the observer who examines it; and so does Kabbalah. But Kabbalah makes an even bolder statement: even the Creator, the Maker of reality, is within the observer.

These earthshaking concepts and more are eloquently introduced so that even readers new to Kabbalah or science will easily understand them. So if you are curious about why you are here, what life means, and what you can do to enjoy it more, this book is for you.

From Chaos to Harmony

Many researchers and scientists agree that the ego is the reason behind the perilous state our world is in today. Laitman's groundbreaking book not only demonstrates that egoism has been the basis for all suffering throughout human history, but also shows how we can turn our plight to pleasure.

The book contains a clear analysis of the human soul and its problems, and provides a "roadmap" of what we need to do to once again be happy. *From Chaos to Harmony* explains how we can rise to a new level of existence on personal, social, national, and international levels.

Kabbalah for Beginners

Kabbalah for Beginners is a book for all those seeking answers to life's essential questions. We all want to know why we are here, why there is pain, and how we can make life more enjoyable. The four parts of this book provide us with reliable answers to these questions, as well as clear explanations of the gist of Kabbalah and its practical implementations.

Part One discusses the discovery of the wisdom of Kabbalah, and how it was developed, and finally concealed until our time. Part Two introduces the gist of the wisdom of Kabbalah, using ten easy drawings to help us understand the structure of the spiritual worlds, and how they relate to our world. Part Three reveals Kabbalistic concepts that are largely unknown to the public, and Part Four elaborates on practical means you and I can take, to make our lives better and more enjoyable for us and for our children.

INTERMEDIATE

Disclosing a Portion: the inner mechanics of the Torah

The fascinating odyssey that is the Pentateuch (also known as the "Torah") contains an ocean of wisdom that can alter reality itself. *Disclosing a Portion: the inner mechanics of the Torah* uncovers that wisdom in a manner no other book has done before.

As you read, you will discover that each protagonist in the stories we know is really a living force within, directing and determining your path in life. When you discover them, you discover your true self. Delve into the text to enrich and empower yourself as you become the happy, confident person that you dream of being.

The Kabbalah Experience

The depth of the wisdom revealed in the questions and answers within this book will inspire readers to reflect and contemplate. This is not a book to race through, but rather one that should be read thoughtfully and carefully. With this approach, readers will begin to experience a growing sense of enlightenment while simply absorbing the answers to the questions every Kabbalah student asks along the way.

The Kabbalah Experience is a guide from the past to the future, revealing situations that all students of Kabbalah will experience at some point along their journeys. For those who cherish every moment in life, this book offers unparalleled insights into the timeless wisdom of Kabbalah.

The Path of Kabbalah

This unique book combines beginners' material with more advanced concepts and teachings. If you have read a book or two of Laitman's, you will find this book very easy to relate to.

While touching upon basic concepts such as perception of reality and Freedom of Choice, The Path of Kabbalah goes deeper and expands beyond the scope of beginners' books. The structure of the worlds, for example, is explained in greater detail here than in the "pure" beginners' books. Also described is the spiritual root of mundane matters such as the Hebrew calendar and the holidays.

ADVANCED

The Science of Kabbalah

Kabbalist and scientist Rav Michael Laitman, PhD, designed this book to introduce readers to the special language and terminology of the authentic wisdom of Kabbalah. Here, Rav Laitman reveals authentic Kabbalah in a manner both rational and mature. Readers are gradually led to understand the logical design of the Universe and the life that exists in it.

The Science of Kabbalah, a revolutionary work unmatched in its clarity, depth, and appeal to the intellect, will enable readers to approach the more technical works of Baal HaSulam (Rabbi Yehuda Ashlag), such as The Study of the Ten Sefirot and The Book of Zohar. Readers of this book will enjoy the satisfying answers to the riddles of life that only authentic Kabbalah provides. Travel through the pages and prepare for an astonishing journey into the Upper Worlds.

Introduction to the Book of Zohar

This volume, along with *The Science of Kabbalah*, is a required preparation for those who wish to understand the hidden message of *The Book of Zohar*. Among the many helpful topics dealt with in this text is an introduction to the "language of roots and branches," without which the stories in *The Zohar* are mere fable and legend. *Introduction to the Book of Zohar* will provide readers with the necessary tools to understand authentic Kabbalah as it was originally meant to be—as a means to attain the Upper Worlds.

The Book of Zohar: annotations to the Ashlag commentary

The Book of Zohar is an age-old source of wisdom and the basis for all Kabbalistic literature. Since its appearance, it has been the primary, and often only source used by Kabbalists.

Written in a unique and metaphorical language, *The Book of Zohar* enriches our understanding of reality and widens our worldview. Rav Yehuda Ashlag's unique *Sulam* (Ladder) commentary allows us to grasp the hidden meanings of the text and "climb" toward the lucid perceptions and insights that the book holds for those who study it.

GOOD FOR ALL

The Secrets of the Eternal Book

The Five Books of Moses (The Torah) are part of the all-time bestselling book, The Bible. Ironically, the Bible is an encoded text. Beneath it lies another level, a hidden subtext that describes the ascent of humanity toward its highest level—the attainment of the Creator.

The Secrets of the Eternal Book decodes some of the Bible's most enigmatic, yet oft-cited epochs, such as the story of Creation, and the Children of Israel's exodus from Egypt.

The author's lively and easygoing style makes for a smooth entrance into the deepest level of reality, where one changes one's world simply by contemplation and desire.

The Kabbalist: a cinematic novel

At the dawn of the deadliest era in human history, the 20th century, a mysterious man appeared carrying a stern warning for humanity and an unlikely solution to its suffering. In his writings, Kabbalist Yehuda Ashlag described in clarity and great detail the wars and upheavals he foresaw, and even more strikingly, the current economic, political, and social crises we are facing today. His deep yearning for a united humanity has driven him to unlock *The Book of Zohar* and make it—and the unique force contained therein—accessible to all.

The Kabbalist is a cinematic novel that will turn on its head everything you thought you knew about Kabbalah, spirituality, freedom of will, and our perception of reality. The book carries a message of unity with scientific clarity and poetic depth. It transcends religion, nationality, mysticism, and the fabric of space and time to show us that the only miracle is the one taking place within, when we begin to act in harmony with Nature and with the entire humanity.

Unlocking the Zohar

The greatest Kabbalist of the 20th century, Rav Yehuda Ashlag (1884-1954) paved a new way for us by which we can reveal the secrets of *The Book of Zohar*. He wrote the *Sulam* [Ladder] commentary and four introductions to the book, in order to help us understand the forces that govern our lives, and to teach us how we can assume control over our destinies.

Unlocking the Zohar is an invitation to a wondrous journey to a higher world. The author, Kabbalist Dr. Michael Laitman, wisely ushers us into the revelations of the *Sulam* commentary. In so doing, Laitman helps us fine-tune our thoughts as we read in *The Zohar*, to maximize the spiritual benefit derived from reading it.

Dr. Laitman also included numerous inspiring quotes from *The Book of Zohar*, specifically translated, edited, and compiled for easy reading and understanding of this powerful text.

The Point in the Heart: A Source of Delight for My Soul

The Point in the Heart; a Source of Delight for My Soul is a unique collection of excerpts from a man whose wisdom has earned him devoted students in North America and the world over. Michael Laitman is a scientist, a Kabbalist, and a great thinker who presents ancient wisdom in a compelling style.

This book does not profess to teach Kabbalah, but rather gently introduces ideas from the teaching. *The Point in the Heart* is a window to a new perception. As the author himself testifies to the wisdom of Kabbalah, "It is a science of emotion, a science of pleasure. You are welcome to open and to taste."

Attaining the Worlds Beyond

From the introduction to *Attaining the Worlds Beyond*: "'Not feeling well on the Jewish New Year's Eve of September 1991, my teacher called me to his bedside and handed me his notebook, saying, 'Take it and learn from it.' The following morning, he perished in my arms, leaving me and many of his other disciples without guidance in this world.

"He used to say, 'I want to teach you to turn to the Creator, rather than to me, because He is the only strength, the only Source of all that exists, the only one who can really help you, and He awaits your prayers for help. When you seek help in your search for freedom from the bondage of this world, help in elevating yourself above this world, help in finding the self, and help in determining your purpose in life, you must turn to the Creator, who sends you all those aspirations in order to compel you to turn to Him.'"

Attaining the Worlds Beyond holds within it the content of that notebook, as well as other inspiring texts. This book reaches out to all those seekers who want to find a logical, reliable way to understand the world we live in. This fascinating introduction to the wisdom of Kabbalah will enlighten the mind, invigorate the heart, and move readers to the depths of their souls.

Bail Yourself Out

Bail Yourself Out: how you can emerge strong from the world crisis introduces several extraordinary concepts that weave into a complete solution: 1) The global crisis is essentially not financial, but *psychological*: People have stopped trusting each other, and where there is no trust there is no trade, but only war, isolation, and pain. 2) This mistrust is a result of a *natural process* that's been evolving for millennia and is culminating today. 3) To resolve the crisis, we must first *understand* the process that created the alienation. 4) The first, and most important, step to understanding the crisis is to *inform* people about this natural process through books, such as *Bail Yourself Out*, TV, cinema, and any other means of communication. 5) With this information, we will *"revamp"* our relationships and build them on trust, collaboration, and most importantly, care. This mending process will guarantee that we and our families will prosper in a world of plenty.

Basic Concepts in Kabbalah

This is a book to help readers cultivate an approach to the concepts of Kabbalah, to spiritual objects, and to spiritual terms. By reading and re-reading in this book, one develops internal observations, senses, and approaches that did not previously exist within. These newly acquired observations are like sensors that "feel" the space around us that is hidden from our ordinary senses.

Basic Concepts in Kabbalah is intended to foster contemplation of spiritual terms. Once we are integrated with these terms, we can begin to see the unveiling of the spiritual structure that surrounds us, almost as if a mist has been lifted. It is a book for those who wish to awaken the deepest and subtlest sensations they can possess.

Children of Tomorrow: Guidelines for Raising Happy Children in the 21st Century

Children of Tomorrow is a new beginning for you and your children. The big revelation is that raising kids is all about games and play, relating to them as small grownups, and making all major decisions together. You will be surprised to discover how teaching kids about positive things like friendship and caring for others automatically spills into other areas of our lives through the day.

Open any page and you will find thought-provoking quotes about every aspect of children's lives: parent-children relations, friendships and conflicts, and a clear picture of how schools should be designed and function.

The Wise Heart: Tales and allegories by three contemporary sages

Kabbalah students and enthusiasts in Kabbalah often wonder what the spiritual world actually feels like to a Kabbalist. *The*

Wise Heart is a lovingly crafted anthology comprised of tales and allegories by Kabbalist Dr. Michael Laitman, his mentor, Rav Baruch Ashlag (Rabash), and Rabash's father and mentor, Rav Yehuda Ashlag, author of the acclaimed *Sulam* (Ladder) commentary on *The Book of Zohar*. The poems herein offer surprising and often amusing depictions of human nature, with a loving and tender touch that is truly unique to Kabbalists.

TEXTBOOKS

Shamati (I Heard)

Rav Michael Laitman's words on the book: "Among all the texts and notes that were used by my teacher, Rav Baruch Shalom Halevi Ashlag (the Rabash), there was one special notebook he always carried. This notebook contained transcripts of his conversations with his father, Rav Yehuda Leib Halevi Ashlag (Baal HaSulam), author of the *Sulam* (Ladder) commentary on *The Book of Zohar*, *The Study of the Ten Sefirot* (a commentary on the texts of the Kabbalist, Ari), and many other works on Kabbalah.

"Not feeling well on the Jewish New Year's Eve of September 1991, the Rabash summoned me to his bedside and handed me a notebook, whose cover contained only one word, *Shamati* (I Heard). As he handed the notebook, he said, 'Take it and learn from it.' The following morning, my teacher perished in my arms, leaving me and many of his other disciples without guidance in this world.

Committed to Rabash's legacy to disseminate the wisdom of Kabbalah, I published the notebook just as it was written, thus retaining the text's transforming powers. Among all the books of Kabbalah, *Shamati* is a unique and compelling creation."

Kabbalah for the Student

Kabbalah for the Student offers authentic texts by Rav Yehuda Ashlag, author of the *Sulam* (Ladder) commentary on *The Book of Zohar*, his son and successor, Rav Baruch Ashlag, as well as other great Kabbalists. It also offers illustrations that accurately depict the evolution of the Upper Worlds as Kabbalists experience them. The book also contains several explanatory essays that help us understand the texts within.

In *Kabbalah for the Student*, Rav Michael Laitman, PhD, Rav Baruch Ashlag's personal assistant and prime student, compiled all the texts a Kabbalah student would need in order to attain the spiritual worlds. In his daily lessons, Rav Laitman bases his teaching on these inspiring texts, thus helping novices and veterans alike to better understand the spiritual path we undertake on our fascinating journey to the Higher Realms.

Rabash—the Social Writings

Rav Baruch Shalom HaLevi Ashlag (Rabash) played a remarkable role in the history of Kabbalah. He provided us with the necessary final link connecting the wisdom of Kabbalah to our human experience. His father and teacher was the great Kabbalist, Rav Yehuda Leib HaLevi Ashlag, known as Baal HaSulam for his *Sulam* (Ladder) commentary on *The Book of Zohar*. Yet, if not for the essays of Rabash, his father's efforts to disclose the wisdom of Kabbalah to all would have been in vain. Without those essays, few would be able to achieve the spiritual attainment that Baal HaSulam so desperately wanted us to obtain.

The writings in this book aren't just for reading. They are more like an experiential user's guide. It is very important to work with them in order to see what they truly contain. The reader should try to put them into practice by living out the emotions Rabash so masterfully describes. He always advised his students to summarize the articles, to work with the texts, and those who attempt it discover that it always yields new insights. Thus, readers are advised to work with the texts, summarize them, translate them, and implement them in the group. Those who do so will discover the power in the writings of Rabash.

A Sage's Fruit: letters of Baal HaSulam

When the great Kabbalist, Rav Yehuda Leib Halevi Ashlag, author of the *Sulam* (Ladder) commentary on *The Book of Zohar*, had to travel, he would write elaborate letters to his students, providing them with guidance and encouragement. These letters reveal the special relationships cultivated between the great teacher and his students. *A Sage's Fruit: letters of Baal HaSulam* is a compilation of those letters. The unique style and tone that Rav Ashlag uses here offer inspiration and guidance to any seeker of spiritual advancement. Now that they are out, it is unclear how we could perceive spiritual advancement without them.

Gems of Wisdom: words of the great Kabbalists from all generations

Through the millennia, Kabbalists have bequeathed us with numerous writings. In their compositions, they have laid out a structured method that can lead, step by step, unto a world of eternity and wholeness.

Gems of Wisdom is a collection of selected excerpts from the writings of the greatest Kabbalists from all generations, with particular emphasis on the writings of Rav Yehuda Leib HaLevi Ashlag (Baal HaSulam), author of the *Sulam* [Ladder] commentary of *The Book of Zohar*.

The sections have been arranged by topics, to provide the broadest view possible on each topic. This book is a useful guide to any person desiring spiritual advancement.

Let There Be Light: selected excerpts from The Book of Zohar

The Zohar contains all the secrets of Creation, but until recently the wisdom of Kabbalah was locked under a thousand locks. Thanks to the work of Rav Yehuda Ashlag (1884-1954), the last of the great Kabbalists, *The Zohar* is revealed today in order to propel humanity to its next degree.

Let There Be Light contains selected excerpts from the series *Zohar for All*, a refined edition of *The Book of Zohar* with the *Sulam* commentary. Each piece was carefully chosen for its beauty and depth as well as its capacity to draw the reader into *The Zohar* and get the most out of the reading experience. As *The Zohar* speaks of nothing but the intricate web that connects all souls, diving into its words attracts the special force that exists in that state of oneness, where we are all connected.

FOR CHILDREN

Together Forever: The story about the magician who didn't want to be alone

Like all good children's stories, *Together Forever* transcends boundaries of age, culture, and upbringing. Here, the author tells us that if we are patient and endure the trials we encounter along our life's path, we will become stronger, braver, and wiser.

In this warm, tender tale, Michael Laitman shares with children and parents alike some of the gems and charms of the spiritual world. The wisdom of Kabbalah is filled with spellbinding stories. *Together Forever* is yet another gift from this ageless source of wisdom, whose lessons make our lives richer, easier, and far more fulfilling.

Miracles Can Happen: Tales for children, but not only...

"Miracles Can Happen," Princes Peony," and "Mary and the Paints" are only three of ten beautiful stories for children ages 3-10. Written especially for children, these short tales convey a single message of love, unity, and care for all beings. The unique illustrations were carefully crafted to contribute to the overall message of the book, and a child who's heard or read any story in this collection is guaranteed to go to sleep smiling.

The Baobab that Opened Its Heart: and Other Nature Tales for Children

The Baobab that Opened Its Heart is a collection of stories for children, but not just for them. The stories in this collection were written with the love of Nature, of people, and specifically with children in mind. They all share the desire to tell nature's tale of unity, connectedness, and love.

Kabbalah teaches that love is nature's guiding force, the reason for creation. The stories in this book convey it in the unique way that Kabbalah engenders in its students. The variety of authors and diversity of styles allows each reader to find the story that they like most.

CONTACT INFORMATION

1057 Steeles Avenue West, Suite 532
Toronto, ON, M2R 3X1
Canada

Bnei Baruch USA,
2009 85th street, #51,
Brooklyn, New York, 11214
USA

E-mail: info@kabbalah.info
Web site: www.kabbalah.info

Toll free in USA and Canada:
1-866-LAITMAN
Fax: 1-905 886 9697